T0328683

Cambridge Elements ≡

Elements in Pragmatics
edited by
Jonathan Culpeper
Lancaster University
Michael Haugh
University of Queensland, Australia

ADVICE IN CONVERSATION

Corpus Pragmatics Meets Mixed Methods

Nele Põldvere
Lund University and University of Oslo

Rachele De Felice
University College London

Carita Paradis
Lund University

CAMBRIDGE
UNIVERSITY PRESS

Shaftesbury Road, Cambridge CB2 8EA, United Kingdom

One Liberty Plaza, 20th Floor, New York, NY 10006, USA

477 Williamstown Road, Port Melbourne, VIC 3207, Australia

314–321, 3rd Floor, Plot 3, Splendor Forum, Jasola District Centre, New Delhi – 110025, India

103 Penang Road, #05–06/07, Visioncrest Commercial, Singapore 238467

Cambridge University Press is part of Cambridge University Press & Assessment, a department of the University of Cambridge.

We share the University's mission to contribute to society through the pursuit of education, learning and research at the highest international levels of excellence.

www.cambridge.org
Information on this title: www.cambridge.org/9781009054515

DOI: 10.1017/9781009053617

First published 2022

A catalogue record for this publication is available from the British Library.

ISBN 978-1-009-05451-5 Paperback
ISSN 2633-6464 (online)
ISSN 2633-6456 (print)

Advice in Conversation

Corpus Pragmatics Meets Mixed Methods

Elements in Pragmatics

DOI: 10.1017/9781009053617
First published online: October 2022

Nele Põldvere
Lund University and University of Oslo

Rachele De Felice
University College London

Carita Paradis
Lund University

Author for correspondence: Nele Põldvere, nele.poldvere@englund.lu.se

Abstract: This Element is a contribution to a new generation of corpus pragmatics research by taking as its starting point the multifaceted nature of speech acts in conversation, and by adopting a mixed-methods approach. Through a unique combination of theoretical, qualitative, quantitative, and statistical approaches, it provides a detailed investigation of advice-giving and advice uptake in relation to (i) the range of constructions used to give advice in different discourse contexts and at different points in time, and (ii) their interaction with dialogic and social factors of advice uptake as key components of frames of advice exchanges in natural conversation. Using data from the London–Lund Corpora of spoken British English, the Element shows, firstly, that there are systematic differences in advising between discourse contexts over the past half a century, and, secondly, that *who* gave the advice and *how* they did it are the strongest predictors of the advisee's response. This title is also available as Open Access on Cambridge Core.

Keywords: advice uptake, speech acts, spoken interaction, language change, London–Lund Corpora

ISBNs: 9781009054515 (PB), 9781009053617 (OC)
ISSNs: 2633-6464 (online), 2633-6456 (print)

Additional resources for this publication at www.cambridge.org/advice

Contents

1 Introduction

Using corpus data of natural spontaneous conversation in different situations, contexts, and times, this Element explores the speech act of advice. We see advice as emblematic of the two fundamental collaborative motives and behaviours of human socialising – helping and sharing – posited by Tomasello (2008). Helping has two directions of fit in human communication, namely, from you-to-me and from me-to-you. Requesting help has a directional fit from you-to-me and is expressed for the benefit of me as the request maker, while advising (and informing more generally) involves offering help and has a fit from me-to-you and is for the benefit of you, that is, the advisee. Tomasello also posits a human collaborative motive of sharing of feelings and attitudes. We see sharing of feelings and attitudes as omnipresent in human communication and intertwined with the basic communicative helping motives.

Helping and sharing through advice in spoken communication more specifically can be conveyed in many different ways and forms. When we began to explore advice, there was no a priori operational definition of advice to engage with for our corpus pragmatic study of spoken dialogue across a range of communicative contexts. The task of identifying instances of advice in the great outdoors posed many challenges, requiring a thorough annotation protocol and meticulous coding procedures. In this Element, advice sequences are dialogic activities because they comprise a sequence of *advice-giving* by an adviser and *advice uptake* by an advisee, and possibly even another act if the advice has been solicited. A crucial component of advice is that it concerns some future action, thought, or behaviour, which the speaker attempts to bring about. The advisee is the main undertaker as well as the main benefactor of that action, but depending on the situation, the adviser's involvement may be required for a successful outcome. These subtle meaning differences of advice are reflected in the formal properties of the advice-giving utterances, which convey different degrees of deontic and epistemic authority on the part of the adviser. The types of constructions used by the speakers offer different affordances for the uptake of the advice, and so the choice of constructions is crucial. Furthermore, the social power relations between the interlocutors must be considered alongside these and a range of other linguistic and contextual factors. Advice-giving may be seen as rewarding for the advisee, but it is still a sensitive undertaking that may be resisted, rejected, or responded to in other ways. If unsuccessful, the advice itself, or the realisation of the advice in an inappropriate context, may have negative consequences for the relationship between the interlocutors. The exchange in (1) between two friends, taken from the London–Lund Corpus 2 (LLC–2) of spoken British English, illustrates these points.

(1)   A: you could use your Club Card uh no Colonel Card thing
           B: but I won't

In (1), speaker A's utterance to 'use your Colonel Card thing' is unambiguously framed as advice directed to B, that is, from me-to-you, albeit with a verb indicating possibility rather than obligation or necessity (*could* rather than *must* or *need to*). This acknowledges the option of declining, which is indeed the case; B outright rejects the advice, with a bluntness that is licensed by the informal and friendly relationship between the interlocutors. In a different setting, these aspects – the form of the advice, of the response, and the effect of either of these on the interlocutors – would be likely to take a different shape.

This complex nature of advice calls for a broad definition of the phenomenon, and for this reason, we conceive of advice as a cover term for a network of instantiations of directive–commissive speech acts that are closely related to each other in terms of their force, direction of fit, and form–meaning properties (see Section 2.1 for details). Previous research on advice has mainly been carried out within the frameworks of Conversation Analysis and traditional corpus linguistics (e.g., Adolphs, 2008; Couper-Kuhlen & Thompson, 2022; Figueras Bates, 2020; Hepburn & Potter, 2011; Heritage & Sefi, 1992; Jefferson & Lee, 1981; Pudlinski, 2002; Stivers *et al.*, 2018; van der Auwera & De Wit, 2010) with restrictions arising from the research methods and scope of the respective disciplines. The main focus for conversation analysts has been institutional contexts on the basis of a limited number of advice sequences. In corpus linguistics, there has been research on speech acts in general (e.g., Aijmer, 1996; Deutschmann, 2003; Jautz, 2013; Ronan, 2015), but it has not been aimed at the dialogic sequences of the acts in discourse. The statistical techniques have also been rather limited, often missing out on the multidimensional complexity of how speech acts are conveyed and received. In addition, for advice specifically, there is no research on how it is used in natural conversation from a diachronic perspective, which is what we are also concerned with here.

The approach to advice in natural spontaneous conversation in this Element is a contribution to a new generation of corpus pragmatics research theoretically, methodologically, and with respect to diachronic corpus data of spoken dialogue. The Element combines theoretical insights from Speech Act Theory and frame-based politeness theory with a usage-based, socio-cognitive approach to meaning-making in discourse. Methodologically, it makes use of a mixed-methods modus operandi of qualitative, conversation analytic as well as quantitative procedures and multifactorial statistical analyses. The data are from the London–Lund Corpora (LLC) of spoken British English, comprising the first London–Lund Corpus (LLC–1) from the 1950s to 1980s and the new LLC–2 from 2014 to 2019. An important feature of the dataset is that LLC–2 was carefully compiled to match the size and design of LLC–1 as closely as possible, thus providing a useful resource for principled diachronic comparisons over the past half a century. The Element is guided by three main aims, namely, to

- describe the constructions used to give advice in spontaneous conversation in English in different discourse contexts over a period of approximately fifty years;
- explain the interaction between the constructions and dialogic and social factors, and on the basis of those, formulate predictions for certain frames of advice exchanges and constructional choice by the interlocutors;
- propose a new paradigm for the study of the multifaceted nature of advice in real communication through a unique combination of theoretical, qualitative, quantitative, and statistical approaches to corpus pragmatics.

The intended readership of the Element is students and researchers in corpus pragmatics interested in new ways of investigating speech acts by means of spoken corpora. These students and researchers might be interested in approaches to speech acts where their observations of the communicative functions of the speech acts are based on a large number of examples extracted from different contexts. They may also be interested in considering the interlocutor's behaviour relative to each other and particularly the addressee's response, which is often neglected at the expense of data from large, multimillion-word corpora and numbers from off-the-shelf software tools (for exceptions in research on turn-taking, see Rühlemann, 2017, and on dialogic resonance, see Tantucci & Wang, 2021). Our approach embraces both of these research agendas without compromising the scientific rigour of either, but rather elevating the capacity of corpus pragmatics to provide answers to previously unexplored questions about speech acts in spoken dialogue. We believe that the basic principles offered in this Element – demonstrated through the speech act of advice – are a good first step in that direction and should be useful both for novices and seasoned researchers of corpus pragmatics.

The introductory section has so far presented the general topic of advice which this Element explores in natural spontaneous conversation. In the next section, we offer a brief overview of the terms and notions of the framework within which the Element is situated; more detailed discussions of the theoretical background are given in Section 2.

1.1 Terms and Notions of Framework

The research on advice in this Element is situated within the usage-based, socio-cognitive approach to meaning-making in discourse. It rests on the basic assumption that meanings are evoked on the occasion of use in the communicative situation. Meaning in language is pragmatic in nature and includes both knowledge of the world and knowledge of language itself. Communication through language is social action through which speakers attempt to change the cognitive status of their interlocutors in one way or another. This means that utterances do not exist in a vacuum but are construed with the aim of achieving the interlocutors' goals and to arrive at a satisfactory level of mutual understanding through a process of meaning negotiation in discourse. In dialogue, speakers co-construct the communicative event and take turns at managing and developing the communicative flow and the outcome of the different speech acts.

These basic assumptions entail a highly dynamic and flexible approach to meaning-making in language, which presupposes that the way in which interlocutors give and receive advice is couched in various layers of cultural knowledge, beliefs, attitudes, and patterns of practice. Following Fillmore (1982) and Fillmore and Baker (2009), we see these layers as the *frame* of the advice act. Frames are culturally based conventionalised knowledge that is shared in a given community. They may include sets of events, for instance, conducting a medical session or running a meeting in a workplace, but events may also be activities related to the act of giving and receiving advice. To elucidate how our research should be understood, we present an outline of what underlies the use of advice constructions in Figure 1.

Figure 1 shows the layers embedded in an advice event and illustrates our theoretical approach to the meaningful functioning of language in this Element. The socio-cognitive frame is the envelope in which the whole advice event is enclosed. It comprises interlocutors' experiences, beliefs, and knowledge about attitudes and social conventions that apply in a given situation. In dialogue, there are at least two frames that cover the experiences and knowledge contributed by the participants in the event. Socio-cognitive frames are important because they form the basis for how advisers construe their utterances and how they negotiate their meanings in the advice act. Important factors that regulate their choices are where, when, why, and with whom they communicate (e.g., professionally or not, formal or informal, age, gender, power relations, cultural background). The discursive frame for advice involves the turn-taking practice of giving and taking. For a successful outcome of the communicative event, the participants need to construct a common ground, that is, a shared workspace of discourse-relevant facts and behaviour (Clark, 1996). Most types of dialogic situations are in a constant flux in natural conversation. Therefore, participants must be flexible and adaptive in the interactive work of upholding the joint activity

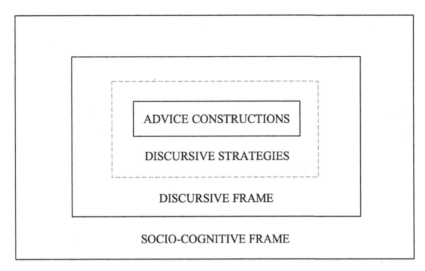

Figure 1 Schematic representation of the various frames and strategies embracing advice constructions

of advice and the constant negotiation of meanings and intentions, as described further in Section 2.2.

Next, in terms of politeness, interlocutors make use of different discursive strategies depending on socio-cognitive and discursive frames in light of what they want to convey in the best way possible. Ideally, these discursive strategies of dialogue are governed by the cooperative principle (Grice, 1975) and an understanding of the participants' needs and requirements in terms of respect for each other's personae and self-esteem, that is, their *face* (Brown & Levinson, 1987; Goffman, 1967). This is where the psychological processes and the discursive strategies related to the intersubjective relationship between the participants become relevant. Goffman refers to face as 'the positive social value a person effectively claims for himself' (Goffman, 1967:5) through their interactions with others. Culpeper and Haugh (2014) adopt a social interdependence view of the notion: we have a certain view of our face, which is affected by how others see us, as demonstrated by their behaviour towards us. There is a general expectation in interaction that interlocutors will tend to minimise behaviour that devalues each other's face, and perhaps even add value to it instead. In Section 2.3.1, we describe how giving and responding to advice are forms of interaction with a high risk of threat to face, and Section 2.3.2 introduces Terkourafi's (2005, 2015) ecological research on face and politeness to increase our understanding of how sociocultural frames interact with cognitive and interactional frames in real communication. Finally, at the core of an advice event we find the advice constructions. We use the term construction in the technical sense, that is, as a synonym for form–meaning pairings in language (Goldberg, 2006).

As previously mentioned, advisers have at their disposal a range of constructions to set the scene so that the advice will appeal to the advisee. According to Searle (1969), there are two types of speech acts, *direct* and *indirect* ones. The definition of a direct speech act is that there is a conventionalised match between sentence type and the illocutionary function of the speech act (declaratives/ assertions, interrogatives/questions, imperatives/directives). There are also a number of performative expressions that are markers of speech acts, for instance, *state/ask/order* (see Levinson, 1983:264, 273 for what he termed the literal force hypothesis). In the case of directives, this canonical form–function status is given to utterances such as *I hereby order/advise you to make an appointment with the doctor*, or to imperatives with the same illocutionary function: *make an appointment with the doctor*. It should be noted, however, that Searle himself did not subscribe to the literal force hypothesis as a basis for his assumptions about meaning in language; in fact, he argued against the literal meanings of sentences, but made use of the idea as a practical analytical tool in his categorisation of utterances in terms of form. In terms of illocutionary force, he invoked his set of felicity conditions for the categorisation (see Section 2.1 for the felicity conditions for advice).

In our usage-based, socio-cognitive framework, we do not assume that sentence types by default are reflexes of directness of illocutionary function, and that all other constructions are indirect illocutionary acts and therefore need special treatment since they are not literal according to traditional work in pragmatics (see also Paradis, 2003a, 2015; Põldvere & Paradis, 2019, 2020). In other words, it is not the case that some utterances are direct, while others are not. Instead, in our framework all constructions that function as advice evoke a representation of that meaning in conceptual space; they are all equally literal. The difference between them is that they may express different degrees of (in)directness, which in our framework is not a matter of form but of intersubjectivity and communicative (in)directness. By communicative directness we refer to utterances that have the effect of contracting the communicative space by making possible a simple response such as *yes* or *no*. Indirectness, however, has the opposite effect of expanding the communicative space and is characterised by a high degree of intersubjective consideration of face to promote successful mutual coordination of mental states. A simple response such as *yes* or *no* in the uptake by the advisee is infelicitous in the case of advice presented in an indirect way. Section 4.1.1 will apply this reasoning to real examples of the advice events investigated in this Element.

The rest of the Element is organised as follows. Section 2 explains the role of advice and other related speech acts within the broad network of instantiations of directive–commissive speech acts. We explain why advice serves as an appropriate test bed for our approach to speech acts, one that takes into account its cognitive, dialogic, and social grounding in real communication from a synchronic as well as a diachronic perspective. Section 3 explains the methodological aspects of the approach, namely, the mixed-methods approach involving qualitative, quantitative, and statistical techniques. We introduce a new resource for studying pragmatic phenomena at different points in time in recent history: the LLC of spoken British English. Section 4 presents the empirical results of the investigation, first focusing on the constructions used to give advice and then on the range of factors that affect the uptake of the advice, followed by a discussion of the theoretical implications of the results for corpus pragmatics in Section 5. Finally, Section 6 concludes the investigation.

2 Background

This section engages with the literature on relevant aspects of advice. Section 2.1 discusses the notion of the speech act of advice and its relation to other types of directive and commissive speech acts such as suggestions, recommendations, offers, and requests. Section 2.2 presents the main lines of research on the practices of advice-giving and advice uptake in various disciplines with a focus on Conversation Analysis and Interactional Linguistics. Finally, in Section 2.3 we outline our understanding of the role of face in interaction, and the advantages of using the frame-based approach to politeness in a corpus pragmatic study of advice specifically and speech acts more generally.

2.1 Advice and Related Speech Acts

The starting point of this Element is Speech Act Theory (Austin, 1962) and in particular Searle's (1969, 1976) taxonomy of speech acts: declarations, representatives, expressives, directives, and commissives. In this taxonomy, advice is an instance of the family of directives together with orders and requests of different kinds. The illocutionary function is the same for all directives, that is, to get the addressee to do something, while the illocutionary force and the direction of fit (from me-to-you or vice versa) may differ among different types of directives. The crucial feature for advice is that the addressee is the main benefactor. This is a feature that advice shares with recommendations and suggestions, but where it differs from orders and requests, which are for the benefit of the person who gives the order or makes the request (i.e., the speaker), and where the direction of fit is from you-to-me.

Table 1 Felicity conditions for the speech act of advice

Conditions	Description
Preparatory condition	A is able to perform the act
Sincerity condition	S believes that it would be good for A to perform the act
Propositional content condition	S predicates future act of A
Essential condition	S attempts to get A to perform the act

Table 1 presents the felicity conditions for the speech act of advice, adapted by us from Searle's (1969) conditions for requests. The four conditions of Table 1 must be fulfilled for a speech act of advice to be felicitous. They are the underlying elements of the activity. The preparatory condition is the situational prerequisite for the speech act, which states that the speaker (S) believes that the addressee (A) is able to perform the act.[1] The sincerity condition states that S genuinely thinks that the piece of advice will be beneficial for A. The propositional content condition relates to what the speech act is about, that is, to predicate some future act of A, and, finally, the essential condition is about S's intention to make A do what S has advised A to do. The felicity conditions were necessary for Searle to account for all types of the form–meaning pairings of advice-giving utterances; therefore, he could also settle the issue of (in)directness and the entailing notion of literalness since the felicity conditions regulate the identification of the speech act irrespective of its form. Performatives such as *I advise you to make an appointment with the doctor*, for example, are direct strategies for giving advice because they have the illocutionary force named by the performative verb in the matrix clause (Levinson, 1983). An advice-giving utterance has to meet all four felicity conditions to be understood as such, irrespective of whether the form of the utterance is direct or indirect. Thus, Searle's classification in particular and Speech Act Theory more generally provides a useful starting point for the analysis of utterances based on their illocutionary function. However, the explosion of methodological reflections on and innovations in research on real communication has highlighted a number of limitations of Speech Act Theory that need to be addressed. Below, we point out three of them that are relevant for the speech act approach developed here.

---

[1] For the sake of comparison with Searle's conditions, we use the terms 'speaker' and 'addressee' to refer to the adviser and advisee in this section, but we make use of the latter terms in the rest of the Element.

The first limitation concerns the fact that, in real communication, speech acts have fuzzy boundaries and therefore strict classification of utterances into Searle's taxonomy is challenging, if not impossible. Directives are not the only speech act that attempts to bring about some future action or that includes A as the intended benefactor, as these properties are also shared by commissives; consider, for example, offers (e.g., *what if I do a roast dinner*). The main difference is that, in the case of offers, the action is carried out by S. Observations of real corpus data, however, reveal that the way in which advice is expressed in conversation often includes both S and A, not only as the intended benefactors, but also as the joint undertakers of the proposed action. Thus, Searle's felicity conditions need to be extended to also reflect the commissive aspect of advice. The second limitation regards the central unit of analysis of Speech Act Theory, namely, the sentence or utterance. It means that little attention has been paid to the specific linguistic constructions through which acts are carried out, and their distribution in real communication. Not every instance of advice includes the performative verb *advise*, as suggested by the relatively low number of hits of the verb (5,323) in the 100-million-word British National Corpus 1994 (Diederich & Höhn, 2012:340). This second limitation of Speech Act Theory sheds light on the third one. The focus on the utterance as the central unit of analysis, as well as on the illocutionary function of single utterances, has meant that the utterances have been considered outside of their dialogic and sequential context. Such considerations are, however, important because they relate to the perlocutionary effect of speech acts or the effect that speech acts have on A's actions. Perlocutionary acts may be external to locutionary acts, but even if accompanied by appropriate intentions, a successful act of advising has not occurred until A (or A and S) has performed the act in question (e.g., sat down, taken a cup of coffee, applied for a job). It is most likely because of the difficulty of actually determining the events that have (or have not) taken place in response to the speech act that the investigation of perlocutionary acts has not taken off in Speech Act Theory. However, one way to resolve this is to turn our attention to the *linguistic* manifestation of advice uptake, that is, how people use language to convey their intentions and reactions. We will return to this point in Section 2.2.

The purpose of this section is to address the first limitation, namely, the relation of advice to other speech acts, and to provide a sufficiently broad, yet operational, definition of advice for our purposes. The standard definition of advice in conversation analytic and interactional linguistic research is that advice 'describes, recommends or otherwise forwards a preferred course of future action' (Heritage & Sefi, 1992:368). This definition covers all the felicity conditions for advice as described in Table 1, and, pending certain clarifications, it has the potential to provide an operational description of advice for analysis in different contexts by different constellations of people. In addition to the speech act of advice, for example, the definition allows for the inclusion of speech acts that are not only directive in nature but also commissive. This is because the definition does not specify who should carry out the future action, thus leaving open the interpretation that A does not have to act alone, but that S may also be involved in some way. Proposals fit into this mould (e.g., *we should do something for Halloween*) and so do certain instances of advice proper, where S makes an explicit reference to herself but where the main undertaker of the action is clearly A. Consider, for example, the utterance in (2), where a supervisor advises a supervisee on her thesis on phonetics. The example is from LLC–2.

(2)   and then we could go into those and uhm make uhm like measurements of
         burst frequency

The intended benefactor of the action is left equally unspecified in the definition, suggesting that both S and A may take on this role. By making an explicit reference to herself in (2), for example, the supervisor constructs a common ground of joint interests and activities where she shares with the supervisee some of the responsibility as well as some of the rewards of a successful thesis. While this move is likely to reduce the level of imposition of the advice act (see Section 4.1.1), it has the same illocutionary function as utterances directed at the addressee only (*you could go into* ...). Therefore, in this Element we use advice as a cover term for the broad network of instantiations of directive–commissive speech acts, which all share the felicity conditions in Table 2 (an expanded version of Table 1). In addition to clear instances of advice (e.g., *I advise you to* ...), the felicity conditions in the table also cover recommendations, suggestions, and proposals (see Section 3.3 for more examples).

Having established a working definition of the speech act of advice in this Element, the next section explores advice from the perspective of

Table 2 Felicity conditions for advice as a directive–commissive speech act

Conditions	Description
Preparatory condition	A or S and A are able to perform the act
Sincerity condition	S believes that it would be good for A or S and A to perform the act
Propositional content condition	S predicates future act of A or S and A
Essential condition	S attempts to get A or S and A to perform the act

constructional choice and dialogic behaviour, thus addressing the second and third limitations of Speech Act Theory above. It reviews literature on the topics of the deontic and epistemic authority of advice constructions as well as how advice is taken up by the interlocutors in different discourse contexts.

2.2 Previous Research on Advice-Giving and Advice Uptake

Advice has received a considerable amount of attention across a range of disciplines, such as linguistics, psychology, communication, education, law, business, and medicine. This diversity has resulted in a wide array of theoretical frameworks, methodological approaches, and practical applications, which often have developed separately across the disciplines (see MacGeorge & Van Swol, 2018 for efforts to consolidate some of them). For practical reasons, we limit the theoretical discussion in this section to disciplines that have produced research with direct relevance to the aims of this Element, focusing on advice research in linguistics and social psychology, and conversation analytic and interactional linguistic approaches to social interaction in particular. These disciplines take as their starting point advice in real communication, attending in a detailed way to the specific linguistic constructions[2] used to carry out the actions of advice-giving and advice uptake, as well as to the systematic organisation of the advice sequences in different contexts. In this way, they provide a suitable ground on which to extend the speech act approach described in Section 2.1 to go beyond the utterance as the primary object of study. At the same time, the focus of these disciplines on qualitative investigations of advice and primarily in institutional contexts opens up a research gap for corpus pragmatics to fill.

In conversation analytic and interactional linguistic approaches to advice, the two fundamental core dimensions of advice are normativity and asymmetry (Heritage & Sefi, 1992). The normative dimension relates to the prescriptive nature of advice whereby the future action is construed as something that the advisee *should* do rather than what they *might* do (i.e., merely delivering information), while asymmetry refers to the relationship between the interlocutors, whereby the adviser is projected as having more knowledge, skills, and experience than the advisee. The dimensions relate closely to the degree of deontic and epistemic authority assumed by the adviser, which is encoded in the specific linguistic constructions used to give advice. According to Heritage (2012), speakers are sensitive to whether or not their contributions are

---

[2] Note, however, that construction in this case is typically not understood in its technical Construction Grammar sense (i.e., a form–meaning pairing), but rather as a syntactic string of words.

informative to addressees and keep detailed score of who knows what, or each other's epistemic domains, in interaction. The focus of this line of research on deontic and epistemic authority explains why much of the research on advice so far has been carried out in professional contexts where asymmetries between the interlocutors are institutionally given, such as medical interaction (e.g., Heritage & Sefi, 1992; Kinnell & Maynard, 1996; Stivers *et al.*, 2018), help lines (e.g., Butler *et al.*, 2010; Hepburn & Potter, 2011; Pudlinski, 2002), student counselling and tutoring (e.g., Vehviläinen, 2001; Waring, 2007), and expert–layperson call-in radio programmes (e.g., Hudson, 1990; Hutchby, 1995).[3]

In her studies of the modal grounding of recommendations in wine reviews, for example, Paradis (2009, 2020) argues that recommendations are weakly deontic in that they foster a middle degree of transfer of the action in the utterance, and therefore are a fruitful ground for the emergence of middle constructions, which foreground the wine and demote the critic who provides the recommendation (e.g., *this beauty should drink well for 10–12 years*). Simultaneously, the middle construction reflects the low epistemic control of the future action talked about and the dissociation of the wine critic from being 'accountable for the correctness of the predictions of the future state of affairs' (Paradis, 2020:114). The critic's deep knowledge and trustworthy sensory abilities are already demonstrated in the socio-cognitive frame and the actual information that precede the recommendation (see also Hommerberg & Paradis, 2014). Similarly, Stivers *et al.* (2018) draw on degrees of deontic and epistemic authority to distinguish between five ways to issue treatment recommendations to medical patients in the United Kingdom and the United States: pronouncements, suggestions, proposals, offers, and assertions. Pronouncements are the most direct expression of medical authority in that they straightforwardly combine both deontic and epistemic dimensions of authority (e.g., *you need to use the cold compresses or ice packs*). In the rest, one or the other dimension is abrogated. For instance, in the case of suggestions, the physician maintains epistemic authority but relinquishes deontic authority (e.g., *you could try Claritin for that*), while in assertions, they 'stand entirely on epistemic ground without an overt leveraging of this authority into a directive for patient action' (e.g., *there are anti-depressant medications that would work very good for you*; Stivers *et al.*, 2018:1340). Thus, the deontic and epistemic properties of advice are useful for establishing a systematic overview of the linguistic constructions that are available to advisers in a given situation, and to classify them according to their strength and speaker confidence.

---

[3] For more professional contexts, see the chapters in Limberg and Locher (2012).

However, the presence of epistemic asymmetry to ascribe deontic or normative properties to advice-giving utterances is much less relevant in contexts where the asymmetries between the interlocutors are not institutionally given, and where the advisers lack the expertise of professionals to give the kind of advice that the advisees would appreciate. This explains why there has been relatively little research done on casual conversation (but see, e.g., Couper-Kuhlen, 2014; Couper-Kuhlen & Thompson, 2022; Jefferson & Lee, 1981; MacGeorge *et al.*, 2016; Shaw & Hepburn, 2013; Shaw *et al.*, 2015). However, advice given in casual conversation may be seen as even more sensitive than in institutional contexts because, to make up for their lack of professional expertise, advisers must pay extra attention to the linguistic constructions they use. Furthermore, since advice is not typically the default aim of such conversations, it might have to be given in ways that are recognisable to the advisee, that is, by using more direct forms. For example, in a recent study of casual conversation between friends and siblings, Couper-Kuhlen and Thompson (2022) examine the five most common formats for advice-giving in American English. They find that the most frequent formats, bald imperatives and the interrogative *why don't you*, are also deontically the strongest advice-giving formats, while the deontically weaker formats, various types of declaratives, are less frequent (see also Couper-Kuhlen, 2014 and MacGeorge *et al.*, 2016 for similar results). By contrast, declaratives make up the largest proportion of the data collected from an online advice column run by a professional organisation as reported in Locher (2013). Specifically, the advice column is characterised by indirect declarative sentences such as those without a linguistically explicit acting subject (e.g., *douching is no longer recommended for a number of reasons;* Locher, 2013:347). However, since Couper-Kuhlen's and Thompson's study was only limited to the five most common advice formats, and Locher's to the full range, it is difficult to make any comparisons between the advice given in casual and institutional contexts at this point.

While it is possible that, in casual conversation, advice is given in more direct ways, this does not necessarily mean that such utterances are well received by the advisee. In a conversation analytic sense, the technically preferred way to respond to advice in the discursive frame is by accepting it (Couper-Kuhlen, 2014:624); however, in real communication advice is often resisted, rejected, or responded to in other ways such as by simply ignoring it (e.g., Couper-Kuhlen, 2014; Couper-Kuhlen & Thompson, 2022; Hepburn & Potter, 2011; Heritage & Sefi, 1992; Jefferson & Lee, 1981; Kinnell & Maynard, 1996; MacGeorge *et al.*, 2016; Pudlinski, 2002; Van Swol *et al.*, 2018). Couper-Kuhlen even goes as far as to say that resistance to advice relates to social order and 'may be a "natural" defense to a social put-down' (Couper-Kuhlen, 2014:635) (see below for the role of solicitation in such settings). Similarly, Jefferson and Lee argue that the advisee's choice to accept, resist, or reject the advice is largely an interactional matter, 'produced by reference to the current talk', more or less independent of intention to use it, or actual subsequent use' (Jefferson & Lee, 1981:403). Interlocutors have no obligation to reveal their true intentions, and therefore it is entirely possible that the way in which advice is received in conversation is contingent upon the linguistic constructions used to give it, in addition to other factors (see below). Indeed, Couper-Kuhlen and Thompson (2022) found that the strongly deontic formats in their data were met with the highest degree of resistance by the advisee, due to what the authors describe as 'a unilateral resolution to the other's problem'. Specifically, advice given with such strong formats may be treated as a unilateral command that leaves little space for the advisee to determine their own future action. In situations where the interlocutors have a symmetric deontic status (i.e., casual conversation), such formats arguably come across as face-threatening (see Section 2.3 for details on the notion of face). In contrast, when the advice was given using deontically weaker formats such as declaratives, the authors observed less resistance. Presumably this is because such formats do not call on the advisee to accept or reject the advice, but rather to acknowledge or to agree that the action in question would be a possible course of future action. In other words, they invite a bilateral search for problem resolution by treating the interlocutors in more equal terms.

Focusing on yet more indirect advice constructions, namely, advice-implicative interrogatives and assessments, Shaw *et al.* (2015) make a similar observation about the way in which advice is given and received in situations where there is a problematic relationship of authority between the interlocutors. While advice-implicative interrogatives set up an answer as opposed to an acceptance or rejection (e.g., *have you talked to any of the people that you used to hang out with*), advice-implicative assessments guide the advisee towards a preferred course of action by stating what is good and bad (e.g., *I think the agency's a good way to go because at least then they can research*; Shaw *et al.*, 2015:321, 330). Both types of advice constructions allow the advisers to mitigate the normative and asymmetric dimensions of advice-giving by leaving more interactional space for the advisee's contingencies to perform the future action. The authors argue that such constructions are particularly useful in casual conversation where advice-giving has not been 'warranted by an institutional role and is instead more contingent and opportunistic' (Shaw *et al.*, 2015:338), and they call for systematic comparisons of how advice is given and received in casual and institutional conversation. At the same time, they raise questions about the efficacy of advice-implicative actions, which may give the advisee more freedom to exploit the implicit nature of the advice through higher degrees of resistance. Since such constructions were not included in Couper-Kuhlen and Thompson (2022), we do not know if this is in fact the case, thus confirming the need to explore the full range of advice constructions and their relation to advice uptake in this Element.

In addition to the formal properties of the advice-giving utterance, many other factors can be expected to affect advice uptake. One of the most discussed factors in the literature is whether or not the advice has been solicited in the prior discourse. In a well-known study of medical interaction between health visitors and first-time mothers, Heritage and Sefi (1992) observe a striking relationship between advice solicitation and the way in which the advice is received. Specifically, they find that first-time mothers tend to treat the advice as informative only if they have directly requested it through question–answer sequences or if they have detailed an untoward, and potentially problematic, state of affairs. In such cases, the mothers tend to use so-called marked acknowledgements (e.g., *oh right,* in which the first component treats the prior advice as news and the second component marks it as an acceptance). By contrast, unmarked acknowledgements (e.g., *mhm, yeah, that's right*) and assertions of prior knowledge and/or competence (e.g., where the mother is already engaged in the proposed action), both of which are strategies of advice resistance, are the preferred forms of advice uptake in situations of health-visitor-initiated advice, that is, advice that has not been solicited by the mothers. One possible reason for such seemingly counterproductive advice outcomes may be the pessimistic and defensive stance taken by the health visitors with respect to the knowledge and competence of the mothers, which may encourage them to offer anticipatory and pre-emptive advice and thus take away the mothers' chance to seek it themselves (Heritage & Sefi, 1992:411).

The problem with giving advice to a friend or family member after they have expressed a trouble is that advice is not necessarily solicited or expected in such situations (MacGeorge *et al.*, 2016:551). Jefferson and Lee (1981) note that even troubles-telling between people who know each other well may not be seen as advice solicitation, due in part to the confusion on the part of the speaker as to what role to adopt, that of a troubles-recipient or an adviser. While the former role focuses on the troubles-teller and their experiences, the latter role focuses on the problem and its properties. Failing to attend to the requirements for emotional reciprocity in situations where the troubles-teller attempts to preserve the status of the talk as a troubles-telling rather than an opportunity for advice-giving may lead to negative outcomes for the relationship between the interlocutors. This might be another explanation for the high rates of resistance observed in Couper-Kuhlen and Thompson (2022) discussed above, suggesting that the desire to determine one's own future action may be even more apparent in situations where the advice has not been explicitly solicited. Whether or not this is a pattern that can be found in casual conversation more generally will be determined in this Element through comprehensive analyses of advice sequences in both solicited and unsolicited settings, as well as in comparable settings in institutional conversation.

Thus, the way in which advice is received in conversation does not seem to be dependent on any one factor operating in isolation but on the close interplay between linguistic and dialogic factors, all contributing to the outcome with varying degrees of strength and importance. The more of these factors we can incorporate into our analyses using multifactorial statistical modelling, the more successfully we can represent the reality of spontaneous dialogic interaction in all its complexity (see Section 3.3). Next, we explore the social factors that might play a role.

2.3 Face and Politeness

In what follows, we look more closely at the interplay of linguistic, cultural, and historical considerations that underlie the occurrence of advice sequences in discourse. We start by explaining the role of face in interaction (Section 2.3.1) and then describe the frame-based approach to politeness adopted in this study (Section 2.3.2). We also demonstrate the applicability of the frame-based approach to diachronic analyses of politeness phenomena in Section 2.3.3.

2.3.1 Face and Advice

In Section 1.1, we briefly outlined why face is an intrinsic aspect of any kind of interaction; here, we focus on its role in advice exchanges specifically. As the overview of previous research on advice showed, advice-giving and advice uptake are a form of interaction of a 'delicate nature' (Locher, 2013:352) with regard to face considerations. They can damage the self-image of the advisee and can risk changing or unbalancing the existing relationship between the interlocutors. People use a range of discursive strategies to mitigate this risk. The complex relationship between face and advice is evident at every stage of interactions involving advice, as each stage carries identity implications with a potential for damage to face for both interlocutors (Goldsmith, 2000:3). Asking for advice entails devaluing one's own face by admitting need, as well as enriching the adviser's face by identifying them as a valued source of assistance. The adviser needs to consider the advisee's face vulnerability in seeking assistance, while not harming their own face by minimising the display of their own competence. If the advice is rejected, the advisee risks devaluing the adviser's face by disregarding their expertise, while if it is accepted, they risk devaluing their own face by confirming their own lack of competence, although there is also space for enhancing the adviser's face when the advice is appreciated. In the case of unsolicited advice, the potential harm to both interlocutors' face is greater than in situations where the advice is solicited, as the advisee is positioned as someone who not only needs help, but is unaware of it, while the adviser positions themselves as someone who can be seen as intruding uninvited into another person's affairs. These challenges contribute to our analysis of advice solicitation and uptake in Section 4.2.

Notably, this view of face and facework involves an understanding of the socio-cognitive frame for advice, specifically, the relationship between the interlocutors, the context of their interaction, and the identities that they claim for themselves in that context (e.g., competent co-worker, knowledgeable tutor, self-reliant daughter, wise friend). Such social factors need to be considered alongside the specific linguistic constructions used to give advice for a more comprehensive understanding of its effectiveness, which perhaps explains MacGeorge *et al.*'s comment that 'attempts to identify precise linguistic strategies that consistently reduce perceived face-threat have been inconclusive' (MacGeorge *et al.*, 2004:44). The same utterance can be perceived very differently depending on, for example, the age, gender, and relationship of the interlocutors, that is, the social factors considered in this study. To support the interpretation of these utterances, the role of face, and the combination of linguistic, dialogic, and social factors they embody, we turn to politeness theory. Broadly speaking, politeness helps explain interlocutors' linguistic (and non-linguistic) behaviours. In the next section, we describe the frame-based approach to politeness, and how it can provide us with an appropriate framework to account for all the factors at work.

2.3.2 Frame-Based Approach to Politeness

In this Element, politeness is understood as a technical cover term for the choices interlocutors make to preserve other people's self-image as well as their own. Important areas of research include impoliteness, rituals and conventions, cross-cultural differences and similarities, among others. It covers a range of theoretical perspectives in pragmatics and linguistics more broadly, from the earlier approaches focusing on linguistic strategies (Brown & Levinson, 1987; Lakoff, 1973; Leech, 1983) to more recent developments that encompass sociocultural considerations and behavioural norms beyond linguistic forms, and which place more emphasis on the participants' perspective of what is polite rather than the researcher's (e.g., Eelen, 2001; Locher, 2006; Mills, 2003; Watts, 2003). Other scholars have pointed out perceived weaknesses of some of these approaches and sought to bring together the different factors at play; one of the most detailed presentations of these criticisms is given by Terkourafi (2005, 2015). Her view is that theories centred on linguistic forms, such as Brown and Levinson (1987), make undue assumptions about the universal applicability of linguistic strategies without closer consideration of what might be appropriate in specific cultures or social situations (Terkourafi, 2005:238). To account for both linguistic strategies and sociocultural norms in her conceptualisation of politeness, Terkourafi proposes a frame-based approach.[4]

For this approach to politeness, Terkourafi (2002, 2005) develops the notion of Fillmore's frame (cf. Section 1.1) by extending its application to interactional contexts, using it as an explanatory tool to understand how interlocutors might know when something is appropriate to the communicative situation. She argues that speakers' repeated experiences of interactions are abstracted into frames to be called upon again when a relevant situation arises. Specifically, Terkourafi translates this perspective to politeness by positing that regular co-occurrence of forms and contexts over time comes to be perceived as polite, leading to politeness as 'a knowledge of which expressions to use in which situations' (Terkourafi, 2002:197). In other words, politeness includes aware-ness of the expected linguistic formulae to be used in a given situation, with the correct use passing unnoticed and marking the speaker as polite. Face consider-ations remain an important part of the framework, but with the broader focus on one's sense of (public) self, rather than specific distinctions between face threat and face enhancement.

Terkourafi's frames are structures of co-occurring components, where the components include both the actual linguistic forms used and 'social categories such as the sex, age, and social class of the participants, the relationship between them, the setting of the exchange, and whether an act is occurring for the first time or is repeated' (Terkourafi, 2005:247). They are central to her view of politeness-as-conventionalisation (see, e.g., Terkourafi, 2015 for a recent pres-entation of the theory), which moves away from the abstract categorisation of particular linguistic strategies as polite or impolite, focusing instead on their association with specific contexts. She argues that it is conventionalisation, rather than varying degrees of indirectness, that determines perceptions of politeness, such that it is not automatically the case that a more indirect formulation will be considered more polite, especially where this is not a conventionally indirect form backed by repeated use (Terkourafi, 2015:15).

---

[4] Terkourafi is part of what is termed the third wave of politeness theory, where scholars seek 'a middle ground between classic and discursive approaches' (Haugh & Culpeper, 2018:216). Other works in this wave include Culpeper (2016), Haugh (2014), Kádár and Haugh (2013), among others.

In this view, politeness is not seen 'as tentativeness, but as providing outward displays of one's familiarity with the norms governing the current exchange' (Terkourafi, 2015:15), and receiving a positive evaluation from the addressee as an acknowledgement. For example, consider the imperative *Break a leg!*. Out of context, it is a rather aggressive and malicious suggestion, but in the appropriate frame – when someone is about to go on stage – it is the most welcome way to utter a wish of good luck (see also Quirk *et al.*, 1985:831–832 for their treatment of imperatives as being used for a wide range of illocutionary acts, where information about the interlocutors as well as the relative benefit of the action is needed). We see politeness as a theoretical framework through which we can interpret the interplay of linguistic choices and contextual factors involved in advice-giving and advice uptake. The frame-based approach is well placed to support these objectives.

The frame-based approach is also suited for a diachronic study of advice-giving. Terkourafi (2005:251) recognises that not every interaction will take place within a pre-established frame, and that novel combinations of linguistic choices and contextual factors will always arise (what she terms nonce contexts). In these cases, interlocutors will still be motivated by their own and the other's face needs as well as the underlying assumption of politeness (rather than aggression), and they will rely on these for the choice of linguistic forms and their interpretation. Of course, every frame once started as a nonce context that subsequently was repeated and entrenched in the speech community, just like what happens to the use of words (Paradis, 2011). Terkourafi's observation that '[s]ocio-historical conditions determine what is regular' and '[w]hat is regular then gets interpreted as polite' (Terkourafi, 2005:250) points to the importance of the diachronic perspective alongside the synchronic for a more comprehensive understanding of the politeness norms at work in a given situation. The design of our study, with two comparable corpora spanning a period of approximately fifty years, makes us uniquely placed to trace the development of new regularities in advice-giving as social norms change and develop over time. Next, we give a brief overview of the main lines of enquiry in diachronic politeness studies, and how these inform our study.

2.3.3 Diachronic Perspectives on Politeness

As previously mentioned, diachronic politeness studies can play an important role in our understanding of present-day politeness. One of the objectives of this study is to investigate how, if at all, advice-giving may have changed over the past half a century in spoken British English, and what this might tell us, indirectly, about changing politeness norms. We take a similar line to

Culpeper and Archer (2008), who looked at requests in earlier centuries and concluded that the changes in frequency of different forms of requesting are not a sign of speakers becoming more polite, but rather of the conventional modes of performing different speech acts changing in step with broader sociocultural changes. We also use the term 'diachronic studies' in a restricted sense. Although there is a large and growing body of research on historical politeness, that is, how politeness was conveyed at particular points in time (for detailed overviews, see, e.g., Fitzmaurice & Taavitsainen, 2007; Jucker, 2020; Taavitsainen, 2018), we are chiefly interested in the development of politeness phenomena over a period of time. Jucker and Kopaczyk note that 'an overall account of the development of politeness or impoliteness across several centuries is still lacking' (Jucker & Kopaczyk, 2017:433); while we cannot cover centuries of dialogue in this Element, our findings can at least contribute to filling some of the gaps regarding politeness in spoken dialogue in recent decades. In fact, the recent past is not well represented in diachronic politeness studies. A useful starting point is Culpeper and Demmen (2011), who focus on requests and politeness in nineteenth century British English. They suggest that historical and social changes in Britain around the mid-1800s led to a change from collectivism to individualism, with the latter being seen as a positive notion. As a result, politeness culture also shifted to one privileging indirectness and freedom from imposition, to show respect for an individual's needs and abilities over those of the collective. Similarly, Jucker (2020) finds an increase in the use of conventional indirect requests in American English as the twentieth century advances. However, Culpeper and Demmen (2011:76) hypothesise that this type of Victorian individualistic politeness might have been waning in more recent decades.

A different line of enquiry that can yield fruitful insights comes from research on change in modality in Present-Day English (see, e.g., Mair & Leech, 2020 for a detailed overview). Modality – especially deontic modality – is often governed by politeness. In advice-giving, for example, the adviser might opt for a deontically weaker format out of considerations for the advisee's face (e.g., *you could change your shirt* versus *you must change your shirt*). Using a variety of corpora, different researchers have observed the demise of deontically stronger modal verbs such as *must* and the concomitant rise of semi-modals such as *have to* and *need to* in recent British English, covering a time span overlapping with that of the present study. For example, an analysis of the Diachronic Corpus of Present-Day Spoken English (DCPSE), covering the period between the 1960s and early 1990s, finds *must* to have been significantly supplanted by *have (got) to* in deontic use (Close & Aarts, 2010), and a substantial decline of *must, may*, and *shall*, particularly in informal face-to-face conversation (Bowie *et al.*, 2013). However, the authors conclude that there is no neat explanation of underlying factors for these changes (Bowie *et al.*, 2013:91). A similar time period is covered by Leech *et al.* (2009), who look at both written British English (the Lancaster-Oslo/Bergen and Freiburg-Lancaster-Oslo/Bergen corpora; LOB and FLOB, respectively) and spoken British English (subsets of DCPSE taken from the years 1961 and 1991). They, too, find a particularly strong decline in the use of *must* and *may*, and suggest that there are various factors at play: not just an increase in semi-modals, particularly *need to* and *want to*, but also a shift away from *must* towards less dictatorial forms such as *should* (Leech *et al.*, 2009:116). An explanation that is offered in support of this change is the democratisation hypothesis, a general advance towards forms of communication that emphasise 'equality of power' and 'express obligation less directly' (Smith, 2003:259). Expanding the time frame to 1931–2006 and using further additions to the LOB family of corpora, later research has confirmed the general trend of *should* increasing in its use as a deontic modal (Smith & Leech, 2013), although this study looked at written English only. Love and Curry (2021) bring us to the present day by comparing changes in modality in spoken British English using the Spoken British National Corpus 1994 and the recent Spoken British National Corpus 2014. Among the relevant findings of their detailed study, they find evidence of a decreased use of *must, shall,* and *will* between the 1990s and 2010s, as well as, interestingly, a decreased use of *have to* and *want to*. Conversely, they observe an increase in the use of weak modals such as *could, might,* and *would*. The study is unclear with respect to changes in the distribution of modal functions (e.g., deontic versus epistemic), since none of the modals showed a significant trend.

This said, the overall pattern that has emerged from the research briefly summarised in this section on change in recent English sees a movement towards greater indirectness, less imposition, and linguistic forms that shift emphasis away from deontic obligation. It is also evident that language change can be tracked even across a relatively short period of time, especially in spoken dialogue, the most common use of language (Clark, 1996). The diachronic component of our study is a test case for these claims, offering an up-to-date comparison of spoken data about a communicative event which necessarily requires some combination of indirectness, imposition, and deonticity. Furthermore, by focusing on one speech act only, we move beyond the broad categories of deontic and epistemic modality addressed by previous research. This makes it more likely that any changes observed are attributable to changes in politeness norms over time, rather than effects of different communicative events.

3 Data and Methods

In this section, we present the data and the methods of the Element. Section 3.1 presents the methodological approach, namely, corpus pragmatics, which we extend and apply to the study of advice sequences in casual and institutional conversation. In Section 3.2, we introduce the corpora from which the sample for the study was extracted: the LLC of spoken British English. Section 3.3 describes the specific features of the combination of the qualitative and quantitative approaches to the data.

3.1 Corpus Pragmatics

Corpus pragmatics, as the name suggests, brings together corpus linguistics and pragmatics. By relying on comparatively large corpora of naturally occurring language for its data, we avoid the pitfall of using 'invented examples of utterances based on native speaker intuition' (Adolphs, 2008:21), a long-standing criticism of traditional pragmatics research. Furthermore, the tools of corpus linguistics allow for the analysis of larger datasets than typically found in pragmatics research, leading to more robust analyses and subsequent generalisations about the phenomena under study. From this perspective, corpus pragmatics can be seen as the use of quantitative corpus linguistic methods to further our theoretical understanding of phenomena in pragmatics. From a complementary perspective, research in corpus pragmatics relies on the insights of pragmatic theories to interpret the quantitative findings of corpus linguistic investigations.[5]

By focusing on advice, we continue in a line of established corpus pragmatics research. Speech acts are one of the richest areas of research in pragmatics, and this has carried across to corpus pragmatics, too. As the field has developed, there have been corpus-based studies of all the main speech act categories: apologies (e.g., Aijmer, 1996; Deutschmann, 2003; Lutzky & Kehoe, 2016), thanking (Aijmer, 1996; Jautz, 2013), requesting (Aijmer, 1996; Murphy & De Felice, 2019; Wichmann, 2004), recommending (Paradis, 2009, 2020), commitments (De Felice, 2013), expressives (Ronan, 2015), and compliments (Jucker *et al.*, 2008). There have also been a few on advice (e.g., Adolphs, 2008; Figueras Bates, 2020; van der Auwera & De Wit, 2010), but they have focused on specific aspects of advice such as a subset of advice forms (Adolphs, van der Auwera and De Wit) and advice mitigation (Figueras Bates). Furthermore, the quantitative nature of corpus pragmatics aligns with our application of the frame-based approach to politeness. The approach advocates

---

[5] The discipline of corpus pragmatics, which was established relatively recently, is rapidly expanding, including its own journal named *Corpus Pragmatics*. Useful overviews are Taavitsainen et al. (2014), Aijmer and Rühlemann (2015), and Rühlemann (2019).

a 'quantitative methodology that makes minimal a priori assumptions about the interpretation of the data' (Terkourafi, 2005:238), and the elements that inhabit the frames – the linguistic expressions themselves, as well as information about various contextual factors – are easily retrievable from corpora. The empirical stance espoused by the frame-based approach is also in line with the study of a sizeable dataset, as required by corpus pragmatics. The carefully matched design of our corpora (see Section 3.2) means that they retain all relevant contextual information, and the multiple instances of each type of context strengthen the generalisations that can be drawn about form–meaning–context combinations. The features of the corpora enable the construction of a rich set of the frames in operation in a range of advice situations, thus showing how corpus pragmatics and politeness theory can work together to advance our understanding of pragmatic phenomena.

Alongside politeness theory, we turn to further quantitative and qualitative methods to unlock the full potential of corpus studies of pragmatic phenomena. From its inception, corpus pragmatics has been described as a venue for 'the pragmaticians who want to provide a statistical foundation to their findings' (Romero-Trillo, 2017:2). As outlined by Jucker (2018:460), this has mainly manifested itself in the form of descriptive statistics (observing the frequencies of the elements of interest) and monofactorial inferential statistics (assessing the strength of difference in the frequencies of single elements). Perhaps because of the relatively young age of the discipline, there have been very few attempts to go beyond this and to explore the role of more complex statistical techniques in elucidating the multifaceted relationships between language, context, and speakers that are of key interest to pragmatics. Most of these studies tend to deal with phenomena in pragmatics such as discourse markers and turn-taking (e.g., Rühlemann & Gries, 2020, 2021), and interactive alignment and dialogic resonance (e.g., Oben & Brône, 2016; Tantucci & Wang, 2021, 2022), but less so with speech acts (but see Tantucci & Wang, 2018 and Van Olmen & Tantucci, 2022 on expressives, and Flöck & Geluykens, 2018 on requests, which also provides a conversation analytic perspective). We believe that the application of these methods to speech acts in particular, which we use in the present study, is an important step forward in corpus pragmatics research. Another common line of enquiry of corpus pragmatics sees it as the 'synergy of corpus linguistics and Conversation Analysis in order to investigate the organizational level of pragmatics' (Clancy & O'Keeffe, 2015:237), focusing on aspects of spoken language such as discourse markers, turn-taking, and backchannels (see, e.g., Aijmer, 2018 and Clancy & O'Keeffe, 2015 for useful summaries). We argue that this dialogic view of spoken interaction can be embedded further into corpus pragmatic studies to assist in the analysis of a wider range of phenomena such as different speech acts. Thus, with this Element we hope to propose a methodologically expansive take on corpus pragmatics, which combines advanced statistical techniques with the detailed interactional focus of Conversation Analysis.

3.2 The Corpora

The data for the Element come from the LLC of spoken British English, comprising the first LLC–1 with data from the 1950s to 1980s (Greenbaum & Svartvik, 1990; Svartvik & Quirk, 1980) and the new LLC–2 from 2014–2019 (Põldvere *et al.*, 2021). An important feature of the dataset is that LLC–2 was compiled to match, as closely as possible, the size and design of LLC–1. Thus, the corpora can be used separately as resources of contemporary speech at particular points in time or together as a diachronic resource for making principled comparisons of pragmatic phenomena over the past half a century. In this Element, they were used for both purposes.

Both LLC–1 and LLC–2 contain approximately half-a-million words stored in 100 texts (including subtexts) of 5,000 words each. There are several different discourse contexts in the corpora, ranging from dialogic contexts such as private face-to-face conversation to monologic contexts such as public prepared speech. The speakers in LLC are educated adults from the United Kingdom with a concentration of speakers from the London area. The transcriptions have been annotated for a range of spoken features such as pauses, overlaps, and various kinds of non-verbal vocalisations (e.g., laughter). In addition, LLC–1 contains prosodic annotations, for example, of the location and direction of nuclear tones. The lack of prosodic annotations in LLC–2 is compensated for by access to the original audio recordings, which allow for additional analyses by the researcher (see Põldvere, Frid, *et al.*, 2021). In this Element, both the prosodic annotations in LLC–1 and the audio recordings in LLC–2 were necessary for the analysis of advice uptake (see Section 3.3.2).

The sample for the Element was extracted from private face-to-face conversation. Face-to-face conversation is the most common use of language across all cultures and societies in the world (Clark, 1996), and it also fits the objective of the Element to determine the practices and frames of advice exchanges in spoken dialogue. The objective to tackle a broad range of conversational contexts including both casual and institutional talk was met by including data from the two types of face-to-face conversation in LLC: conversations between equals and conversations between disparates. In the corpora, speakers are equal if they are friends, peers in the workplace, or related by descent or partnership (e.g., parent–child, husband–wife). They are disparates if they have

Table 3 The sample used in the study

Corpus	Type of conversation	Number of texts	Number of words
LLC–1	Equals	36	180,000
	Disparates	9	45,000
	Subtotal:	**45**	**225,000**
LLC–2	Equals	30	150,000
	Disparates	15	75,000
	Subtotal:	**45**	**225,000**
	Total:	**90 texts**	**450,000 words**

hierarchically unequal positions in a workplace or an educational institution (e.g., employer–employee, teacher–student). Thus, the conversations between equals correspond roughly to casual talk, while the conversations between disparates are more similar to institutional talk.

Table 3 presents the final sample in terms of the number of texts and words. As we can see in Table 3, the sample is approximately 450,000 words (ninety texts) in size, with the same number of words, 225,000 (forty-five texts), from both LLC–1 and LLC–2.[6] Some differences can be observed at the level of the types of conversation; while fifteen out of forty-five of the conversations in LLC–2 are between disparates, only nine out of forty-five of the conversations in LLC–1 are. This issue is mitigated by the use of inferential statistical techniques; however, as we will show in Section 4, small sample sizes raise an important methodological issue, namely, data sparseness. We know that the number of speakers in the subsample from LLC–2 is 125; unfortunately, this information is not readily available for LLC–1.

3.3 Qualitative and Quantitative Approaches

In what follows, we describe the combination of the qualitative and quantitative approaches to the data. It involved extracting and identifying the advice-giving utterances (Section 3.3.1), annotating them for various factors (Section 3.3.2), and then subjecting them to rigorous statistical analysis (Section 3.3.3). The qualitative approach punctuated the analysis at various steps of the process, ranging from the identification of advice based on its communicative function,

---

[6] Almost all the texts and subtexts of face-to-face conversation from the corpora were included. The only exceptions in LLC–1 were texts S.5.8–S.5.11, S.5.13 and S.6.9, and in LLC–2 we excluded texts T023 and T031. The reasons for the exclusions were to achieve a balanced sample across the corpora, as well as the rigid structure and poor audio quality of some of the recordings.

to the close analysis of how the advice is initiated, constructed, and received in the broader discursive frame, and, finally, to the qualitative interpretation of the output of the statistical models. The interpretation of the findings, in particular, borrowed insights from Conversation Analysis, which, as we showed in Section 2.2, has been extensively used in advice research.

3.3.1 The Extraction and Identification of Advice

The extraction and identification of relevant data is both the core strength and core challenge of corpus pragmatics. Corpora provide a sizeable amount of data that allows for robust findings, but the lack of simple form–function relationships makes the task of extracting the data much harder than part-of-speech tagging or simple lexical searches. Specifically, there is no single way to perform a given communicative function (e.g., an apology can take the forms *sorry, I apologise, it was bad luck*), and the same form can fulfil different functions depending on the context (*sorry* can be an apology, a request for repetition, an invitation to move out of the way). Research in corpus pragmatics follows either a form-first or function-first approach (e.g., Rühlemann, 2019:8). In the former, all instances of relevant (known) forms are extracted using corpus software tools. This approach can be applied to corpora of any size with little effort, but it will necessarily overlook more unusual or creative examples that are not captured by the search terms, thus potentially leaving some areas of the topic unexplored. A function-first approach, on the other hand, prioritises coverage of the pragmatic phenomenon of interest by selecting all its instantiations, regardless of form. This can only be achieved by significant human intervention in the form of pragmatic annotation, which requires manual identification of each instance and is therefore only possible with small-scale corpora, though efforts at automated pragmatic annotation are in early stages of development (see, e.g., De Felice *et al.*, 2013 and Weisser, 2019; for a comprehensive overview of pragmatic annotation, cf. Archer & Culpeper, 2018).

Our study is double-barrelled in that it first adopts a form-first approach and then a function-first approach. The reason for starting with the form-first approach is that the nature of advice-giving is such that there is broad agreement on a set of linguistic forms canonically used for this function, as evidenced by the significant overlap and similarity among the phrases studied in previous work on advice-giving (cf. Section 2.2). These are easily searchable due to their formal predictability. Of course, they do not always yield accurate results, but at least they provide an initial list of candidate examples based on which further manual work can take place (see below). The full list of search terms used in the study is given in Part 1 of the Annotation Manual (available as part of the supplementary material of the Element); here, we provide an overview of the main categories of search terms in Table 4 and describe the main principles that guided our process of constructing the full list.

We began by considering the phrases listed by Couper-Kuhlen and Thompson (2022), as they provide one of the most comprehensive overviews of advice-giving constructions, all of which have formal predictability: imperatives, interrogatives, and different forms of modals. This was motivated by the belief that relying on a previously established set of forms would facilitate comparisons between previous studies and our own. However, a pilot study involving manual read-throughs of a subset of the conversations in the corpora revealed a number of additions to the set of search terms, of two main types. The first consists of the natural grammatical and lexical expansion of the initial set of forms by including either a wider range of subjects (e.g., from second person modal and semi-modal constructions to all subjects), verb choices (e.g., from *have you tried* to *have you* + any verb), or interrogatives

Table 4 Main linguistic categories of search terms for advice; the search terms are underlined

Categories	Examples
• Imperatives	*get back in the habit of writing under timed conditions*
• Interrogative markers	*why don't we go then*
	have you ever looked in other parts of the library
• Modal and semi-modal verbs	*you need to know who he is*
	I would put all three down
• Comparative/superlative adjectives	*better turn your attention to lexicography*
	your best bet is to go to the University Library
• Conditionals	*well if you just write to Paxted College*
• Performative verbs and speech act related nouns and adjectives	*I propose to write saying I'm very sorry*
	there's no point spending extra money on a trigger
• Other markers	*I think it's probably a sensible thing to do*
	like just some Gaviscon

(e.g., from *what about* to *how about*). The second stems from a broader under-standing, arising from our pilot study, of the different parts of speech and constructions that can provide advice, such as nouns (*suggestion, idea*), adjectives and adverbs (*advisable, worth(while)*), and performative verbs (*I recommend*). The pilot study also pointed us towards the inclusion of mitigators and stance markers (e.g., *I think, just*) as a further signal of an advice-giving utterance, ensuring that we took into account all the different components of this kind of speech act, formal and attitudinal. Through this iterative process of combining insights from previous literature, our own understanding of the texts, and simple substitutions and expansions of the terms licensed by the grammar, we have arrived at a comprehensive list of search terms giving us broad coverage of advice-giving in our data. Indeed, often different search terms yielded the same utterance (cf. the conditional with *just* in Table 4), a redundancy which reinforces our confidence in the exhaustiveness of the coverage of the search terms. Naturally, there will be ad hoc or idiosyncratic formulations which will not be captured by our terms. These formulations are highly individual and specific to, and comprehensible within, only a particular conversation. Although such for-mulations might be interesting examples of linguistic creativity, their idiosyn-cratic nature makes them of less relevance for our study, which aims at uncovering frames and generalisable patterns of advice-giving in language.

The procedure of extracting candidate examples of advice based on the search terms above was as follows. The texts were prepared by first removing all XML markup (including descriptions of events such as <event desc= "phone rings"/>) and passages of untranscribable text. Almost all the searches were done using simple command line queries with wildcards allowing for intervening modifiers or false starts (e.g., *you really should*, *what what about driving*). These search terms are syntactically straightfor-ward and belong to a closed set of forms. Imperatives and evaluations (comparative and superlative forms), however, belong to an open set and therefore required part-of-speech tagging and syntactic parsing for their extraction. This was done with a Python script using the *Pattern* package (De Smedt & Daelemans, 2012), which includes a suite of natural language processing tools including part-of-speech tagging and full syntactic parsing. For the evaluations, the former was sufficient: the script identified all instances with words tagged as comparative and superlative adjectives. For imperatives, we had to take into account the lack of a specific part-of-speech tag for imperative forms, which in this model was labelled bare verb (VB), a category which also includes items such as *read* and *go* in constructions such as *I can read* and *he wants to go*. The script thus relied on full parsing of each instance, returning only those where verbs tagged as VB were also lacking in subject, to model the characteristics of imperatives. The nature of spoken language is such that there were many utterances incorrectly identified as imperatives, as in this example: *probably boil them with the spikes.* For the simpler searches, the problems were false starts and repetitions, which returned examples such as *you are you are going to try this* as a result for *are you going to*. The automatically extracted data, then, still required manual intervention and cleaning. The sizes of our corpora allowed us to reap the benefits of both automated and manual approaches: they are large enough to provide a substantial number of examples for robust bias-free generalisations, while just about manageable for human annotators to review and annotate the data, as we go on to describe.

Following the form-first approach, we turned to function by comparing the candidate examples to the felicity conditions of advice established for this study (see Section 2.1). The procedure we followed is outlined in Part 2 of the Annotation Manual. The felicity conditions cover a broad network of instantiations of directive–commissive speech acts. A more detailed breakdown of what the felicity conditions look like in discourse is given in (a)–(f); we consider an utterance to be an instance of advice-giving only if it exhibits all the properties below.

(a) The focus of the utterance had to be on the advisee's action; the adviser had to elicit an action from the advisee, not just communicate their attitudes or values.

(b) The proposed action had to include the advisee as one of its undertakers; the advisee could act alone or jointly with the adviser, but the action could never be carried out by the adviser alone.

(c) The advisee – either solely or jointly with the adviser – was the benefactor of the action.

(d) The action had to take place in the future; references to past actions were not considered.

(e) The utterance had to be directed at people who were present in the conversation at the time of the utterance; reported speech and general statements without a clear addressee were excluded.

(f) When the utterance was ambiguous between advice and another type of speech act such as a general statement, the addressee's response was consulted; the utterance was considered to convey advice if the addressee either agreed or disagreed to carry out the proposed action, rather than simply providing information.

To illustrate the presence or absence of the properties above, the utterances in italics in (3)–(5) were considered to convey advice, while the utterances in

(6)–(8) were not.[7] Example (3) is a clear example of advice-giving. It focuses on a future action intended to be carried out by the advisee to his benefit. Both the adviser and the advisee are present in the conversation, and the advisee's response (*yes*) indicates that he accepts the advice. Example (4), a proposal, also has all the necessary properties. The major difference with (3), however, is that, in (4), both the adviser and the advisee are expected to carry out and benefit from the action. The utterances in (5) are very indirect ways of making suggestions in English; however, the focus is still on the proposed action, that is, to have a Christmas get-together.

(3)   (B is an architect who advises A on a renovation project)

      A: I mean what I'm imagine that we're doing in pulling back to ensure that we can pay for things that we really want is at least getting a good job done on the things that we do get done rather than shaving all over the place . . .

      B: yeah . . . I think that *well my advice would certainly be to you to do structural and constructional alterations*

      A: yes

(4)   A: *oh we should do something for Halloween*

      B: we should

(5)   A: *Christmas is a good excuse maybe to just have an impromptu coffee and mince pie* . . .

      B: that's a good idea *maybe just after the end of the term* but not too long after because otherwise people start disappearing . . .

      A: yeah definitely after term

These properties are not present in (6)–(8). In (6), what is in focus is B's assessment of what might or might not work, rather than a call for action. The offer in (7a) and the request in (7b) did not qualify because of the addressee's lack of involvement in the action and the addressee's lack of benefit, respectively. Finally, in (8) the interlocutors make a series of statements about what constitutes a good lecture by using the second-person pronoun *you*. However, the pronouns seem to be used in a general sense without necessarily being directed at the addressee.

(6)   (The speakers are drawing up a floor plan)

      A: that division doesn't need to be there anymore

      B: oh that doesn't need to be there oh yeah *that could work*

      A: or the door could even open like wham and open like that

---

[7] All the examples in this section are from LLC, unless otherwise indicated. Many of them have been simplified through the exclusion of, for example, pauses, repetitions, and false starts to facilitate the task of the reader. Three dots (. . .) are used to omit irrelevant talk.

(7)   a. *I'll cover your answer in my letter*
           b. *I wonder if I might see you very briefly*

(8)   A: I've never given the same lecture twice yet it's very wearing . . . *you can't do the same thing twice really*
           B: *the beauty of an excellent lecture is you're supposed to be able to give it again* that's what compensation for the sweat of preparing it
           A: that's right but it's not like that with media . . . we haven't got a textbook you see

In addition, we excluded what looked like instructions (e.g., *what have you put on your thing -> you just stick that on the back*). While instructions seem to have all the properties in (a)–(f), according to Leech, they 'tend to have a collaborative illocutionary function, and therefore they lie outside the realm of (im)polite behavior' (Leech, 2014:137). Face and politeness are important aspects of this study, so we decided not to include instructions after all.

The Annotation Manual helped us to be consistent in our annotation decisions and it ensured that the annotators followed the same guidelines. To assess the reliability and replicability of the guidelines, a series of inter-rater reliability tests were carried out based on the annotations of the first author of this Element and the annotations of ~10 per cent of the data by the second author. The inter-rater reliability tests were conducted over three rounds of three corpus texts each, separated by discussion sessions where disagreements between the annotators were discussed and resolved together. The intermediate sessions served to progressively refine the annotation guidelines and address unanticipated problems. All choices made during those sessions were recorded and added to the Annotation Manual, which was then used to revise the rest of the annotations. The results from each annotation round (R) are given in Table 5. We report the values of two measures: observed agreement (in percentages) and Cohen's (1960) chance-corrected kappa.

Table 5 shows that the kappa scores obtained for the identification of advice reached at least substantial levels of agreement across all three rounds, according to the scale of Landis and Koch (1977). The third and final round, in particular, showed the best result ($k = 0.922$, 'almost perfect agreement'), which indicates that the annotation task had become clearer and better defined by the end.

3.3.2 The Annotation of Advice

Following the extraction and identification of the advice-giving utterances in the corpus sample, we performed a close manual annotation of the utterances and their context for linguistic, dialogic, and social factors. The most important of these were presented in Section 2.2 (e.g., form of advice, (non-)solicitation of advice, advisee's response to advice), but there are many other factors typically

Table 5 Inter-rater reliability test results: the identification of advice

	Observed agreement (%)			Cohen's kappa		
	R1	R2	R3	R1	R2	R3
Advice	97	96.2	98.1	0.771	0.721	0.922

not dealt with in the literature that might affect how advice is given and received in conversation (e.g., social factors such as the age and gender of the interlocutors). Table 6 summarises the annotation factors and values. The factors can roughly be divided into three groups. The first group (in light grey) comprises linguistic factors that we used to develop a systematic overview of the constructions used to give advice along varying degrees of deontic and epistemic authority and, by extension, communicative (in)directness, which in turn was the basis for systematic comparisons across time and discourse contexts. The combined values of the linguistic factors also make up the first factor based on which we predict the advisee's response to the advice. This allowed us to determine how, if at all, constructional choice affects advice uptake. The other predictors of advice uptake, dialogic and social factors, are in the second group of factors in Table 6 (in darker grey). The third group (in darkest grey) comprises just one factor, the advisee's response to the advice, that is, the factor to be predicted. It is important to keep in mind that the factors in Table 6 are limited to the types of factors that the corpus data allowed us to consider. Advice uptake may depend on a range of other factors (e.g., comprehensibility, relevance, feasibility, absence of limitations; see MacGeorge *et al.*, 2004); however, these factors are better suited to be tackled by survey and experimental methods than corpus methods. In the following, we provide brief descriptions of each factor and their values. A more detailed overview is given in Part 3 of the Annotation Manual.[8]

We start with linguistic factors, all of which relate to the advice-giving utterance. The first factor, form of advice, stands out because it is open-ended and therefore defies strict classification. This is due to the diverse range of linguistic forms used to give advice, a feature which would have made it difficult for us to impose strict categories on the data. Instead, we identified the part of the advice-giving utterance which contained the main illocutionary message of the utterance. Among the items included are references to the participants involved in the action (typically pronouns), the verb phrase conveying the action, noun phrases and adjective phrases (e.g., comparatives) in the subject and subject predicative positions, question words, negative markers, and

---

[8] Note that the social factors were not included in the manual because they were derived from the corpus metadata and therefore required almost no decision-making.

Table 6 Annotation factors and values

Factors	Values		
Form of advice	[Open-ended]		
Utterance type	Imperative		
	Interrogative		
	Declarative		
	Conditional		
Presence or absence of modifiers	Hedge		
	Emphasiser		
	Stance marker		
	NA		
Type of event	Dynamic		
	Stative		
Deictic time	Immediate		
	Distant		
(Non-)solicitation of advice	Advisee asks for advice		
	Advisee asks for opinion or information		
	Advisee discloses problem		
	Advisee announces plan of action		
	Adviser identifies problem		
	Adviser volunteers advice		
Relationship	Equals		
	Disparates [all combinations]		
Age	[All combinations]		
Gender	[All combinations]		
Advisee response to advice	Acceptance	Commitment to act	
		Positive evaluation	
		Marked acknowledgement	
	Resistance	Unmarked acknowledgement	
		Assertion of prior knowledge/ competence	
	Rejection	Elaborated	
		Straightforward	
	Other	NA	

so forth. If the advice-giving utterance did not contain any such items, the whole utterance was included (excluding modifiers; see below). Examples (9)–(13) illustrate some of the items included (in italics).

(9)   *slow down* your pace a little bit [verb phrase]
(10)   *you should get into* a job as quickly as possible [pronoun, verb phrase]
(11)   I think *your paraphrasing could be better* [noun phrase, verb phrase, adjective phrase, comparative adjective]
(12)   darling *why don't you bribe* Jo to lend you her Cold Comfort Farm [question word, negative marker, pronoun, verb phrase]
(13)   I think *twice a week* [whole utterance]

The next linguistic factor, utterance type, has four values – imperatives, interrogatives, declaratives, conditionals – and concerns the grammatical form of the advice-giving utterance. While imperatives and interrogatives are straight-forward, the distinction between declaratives and conditionals requires some explanation. The distinction lies in the location of the proposed action in the utterance in that, when the action was in the main clause, the utterance was considered to be a declarative (e.g., *if the weather allows you can mow the lawn*), but when the action was in the conditional clause, the utterance was a conditional (e.g., *if we could go to York a few days before that would be really nice*). The advice-giving utterances were also annotated for the presence or absence of modifiers, which were divided into hedges (e.g., *I think, well,* tag questions), emphasisers (e.g., *obviously, always,* intensifier *do*), and other stance markers that mark, for instance, viewpoint, attitude, or focus (e.g., *ideally, honestly, actually*). Importantly, the modifiers had to take scope over the whole advice-giving utter-ance. Taken together, the linguistic factors provide us with enough information about the degree of deontic and epistemic authority of the advice-giving utter-ance, and they also help us to test the prediction that there is a relation between the format of the advice-giving utterance and its uptake.

The dialogic and social predictors of advice uptake in Table 6 go beyond the advice-giving utterance and refer to the broader discourse and sociocultural context. The first two dialogic factors are type of event and deictic time. Type of event refers to the spatio-temporal structure of the proposed action. It has two values: dynamic and stative. While dynamic events include change of state (e.g., *you must start to rearrange your estimates of Lawrence's novels*) and state of change (e.g., *go to the planning and buildings committee*), stative events include state of no change (e.g., *I think that's about the minimum of what would make it worthwhile*). Deictic time is concerned with when the advisee is expected, or is in the position, to carry out the action relative to the time of the utterance. The cut-off point is the present conversation, in which case the deictic time is immediate if the advisee is to carry out the action during the course of the conversation (e.g., *I think weekdays would be pre-ferred* in a context where the advisee has to propose a suitable weekday immediately) and it is distant if the action goes beyond the present conversation (e.g., *this could be held alongside a teaching job* in a context where the decision about taking the job does not have to be made immediately). We associate both factors, type of event and deictic time, with the effort required to carry out the action. Based on the assumption that it is more difficult to change someone's mind than to elicit physical action, and that distant actions are more demanding than immediate actions, we associate dynamic and immediate action with low effort and stative and distant action with high effort. Assuming also that there is a relationship between perception of effort and advice uptake (cf. MacGeorge *et al.*, 2002), we expect dynamic and immediate action to lead to higher levels of acceptance of advice than stative and distant action.

The last dialogic factor, (non-)solicitation of advice, is concerned with the way in which advice is initiated in the preceding context. The values are based on Goldsmith's (2000) typology of six patterns of advice initiation, ordered from the clearest case for advice solicitation to the clearest case for when the advice is not solicited. The first four values are initiated by the advisee, meaning that the person who is expected to respond to the advice is also its initiator. First, when advisees ask for advice, they do so in a relatively explicit way, through clear statements (e.g., *I need your advice*), explicit requests (e.g., *what should I do*), or somewhat narrower questions (e.g., *should we try and get tickets for Duna Jam*).[9] Second, when advisees ask for an opinion on some action (e.g., *what do you think*) or simply for information (e.g., *which was the troubled pear*), the advisability of the action is implied rather than explicitly stated. Third, when advisees disclose a problem, their announcement of the problem may make advice solicitation plausible, as in when they make confessions of ignorance or uncertainty (e.g., *my teaching evaluations were terrible again I really don't know what to do*) or pose rhetorical questions (e.g., *how can I possibly finish all my work before break*). Fourth, when advisees announce a plan of action, they may suggest that the plan is in some way problematic, as in (14).

(14)   A: I'm inserting a new stylus into the record player [advisee announces plan of action]
        B: why not put it into the head [advice-giving utterance]

The last two values are initiated by the adviser, meaning that the person who gives the advice is also its initiator. The first one of these is when advisers identify a problem, in which case the problem and the advice are given in separate turns. Consider (15), where the advisee's acknowledgement of the problem provides a basis for the advice in the next turn. By contrast, the

---

[9] Some of the examples in this paragraph are from Goldsmith (2000).

constructed example in (16) illustrates a situation where the adviser volunteers the advice and where the advice and the problem are in the same turn.[10]

(15)   A: do you have a Young Persons Railcard [adviser identifies problem]
        B: no I don't
        A: you should get one [advice-giving utterance]

(16)   A: do you have a Young Persons Railcard # you should get one [both in the same turn]

Following previous research on the topic, we expect there to be a decrease in the level of acceptance of advice as we move from explicitly solicited advice to unsolicited advice.

The social factors are represented by factors such as the relationship between the interlocutors, and their age and gender. The interlocutors' relationship was determined based on the distinction made in LLC between conversations among equals and disparates. All combinations of the latter were considered: when the addressee was of lower rank, higher rank, and when there were addressees of different ranks. When the interlocutors in conversations between disparates were on the same level, they were considered to be equals instead. A similar principle was followed in the annotation of the age and gender of the interlocutors. The combinations of age included conversations where the advisee was younger, older, when the interlocutors were roughly the same age (± ten years), and when there were advisees of different ages. The combinations of gender included same-gender conversations (male–male, female–female), mixed conversations (male–female, female–male), and when there were advisees of different genders. The relative lack of research on the effects of these three factors on advice uptake makes us hesitant to make any predictions at this point.

Finally, we annotated the advice sequences for the advisee's response to the advice. The factor has four main values – acceptance, resistance, rejection, other response – of which the first three were further divided into sub-values. The choice of the (sub-)values draws on research from a number of studies, most notably, Hepburn and Potter (2011), Heritage and Sefi (1992), Pudlinski (2002), and Shaw and Hepburn (2013). First, when advisees accept the advice, they do so in one of three ways: (i) commitment to act (17), (ii) positive evaluation (18), and (iii) marked acknowledgements, which treat the advice as informative and helpful (e.g., *yes*, *okay*, *oh right*, partial repeats, as well as *yeah* and *mm* with a rising–falling and rising intonation).[11]

---

[10] The hash sign (#) in (16) illustrates a possible tone unit boundary.

[11] We added intonation as a potential indicator of informativeness because of the meaningful functioning of pitch contours, for instance, the association of rising intonation with

(17) A: maybe you should just check to be sure
      B: I will tomorrow morning I'll be checking [commitment to act]

(18) A: like Lost in the City or something
      B: oh that's a good one [positive evaluation]

Second, advice resistance involves cases where the advisee avoids treating the advice as informative and helpful, but where the proposed action is not necessarily rejected. The two types of resistance are: (i) unmarked acknowledgements (e.g., *right*, as well as *yeah* and *mm* with a falling intonation)[12] and (ii) assertions of prior knowledge and/or competence (19).

(19) A: it'd make it easier if you could give them an example of someone else who is doing it right
      B: that's what I'm saying [assertion of prior knowledge]

Third, rejections include (i) elaborated rejections in which case the advisee provides a justification for the rejection (20), and (ii) straightforward rejections where no such justification is provided (21).

(20) A: we can go over and do mine
      B: mm but you wouldn't know how the system works [elaborated]

(21) A: you could use your Club Card uh no Colonel Card thing
      B: but I won't [straightforward]

Finally, other responses include, for instance, silence, laughter, and topic shifts.

To assess the reliability and replicability of the guidelines in this part of the analysis, we carried out two types of inter-rater reliability tests – observed frequency and Cohen's kappa – over three annotation rounds (see Section 3.3.1 for the same procedure). The results of the three annotation rounds are given in Table 7. Note that no measures were obtained for the open-class factor of form of advice, which due to its nature would have required a different approach. Also, the disagreements associated with this factor were so minor that they had little effect on the development of the constructional overview in Section 4.1.1.

Overall, the results in Table 7 suggest that the guidelines for annotating advice in this study were clear and well defined. The kappa scores were especially high in the case of utterance type, type of event, and deictic time

---

inconclusiveness, uncertainty, and openness to input, and rising–falling intonation with surprise (Cruttenden, 1997; Paradis, 2003b).

[12] Falling intonation is associated with conclusiveness, certainty, and finality (Cruttenden, 1997; Paradis, 2003b), which in advice situations may mean that the advisee has already made up their mind about the problem.

Table 7 Inter-rater reliability test results: linguistic, dialogic, and social factors

	Observed agreement (%)			Cohen's kappa		
	R1	**R2**	**R3**	**R1**	**R2**	**R3**
Utterance type	95.8	100	100	0.911	1	1
Modifiers	87.5	85	95.2	0.774	0.729	0.913
Type of event	95.8	95	97.6	0.903	0.828	0.95
Deictic time	95.8	100	100	0.915	1	1
Solicitation	95.8	70	88.1	0.945	0.577	0.849
Response	75	80	85.7	0.668	0.748	0.756

('almost perfect' or 'perfect' agreement across all three rounds). Somewhat lower levels of agreement were obtained for the presence or absence of modifiers, although the good result obtained in the last round shows that the problems encountered earlier in the annotation task had been resolved by the end of the rounds. Perhaps unsurprisingly, the kappa scores were lowest for (non-)solicitation of advice and advisee response to advice, both of which are factors that are inherently subjective and context dependent. Those factors were also most sensitive to the types of texts that were analysed in each round. Texts with many instances of advice were more challenging than texts with only a couple of instances of advice, because it was difficult to determine in each case whether or not the advice was solicited, or which response should be considered. Conducting the annotations over several rounds helped us to become more aware of the influence of such confounding biases (see also Põldvere *et al.*, 2016).

3.3.3 Statistical Analysis

The multifactorial nature of our data requires the use of advanced statistical analyses. So far, the norm in pragmatics research has been to rely on simple monofactorial analyses, which work well in cases with only one potential cause-effect relationship but are less suited in situations where the cause–effect relationship is expected to be moderated by multiple factors, which simultaneously amplify and downplay each other's effects. In fact, it is the latter scenario that is believed to be the situation in linguistics (Gries, 2015a:175), as is also evident from the growing number of multifactorial analyses in corpus pragmatics (e.g., Oben & Brône, 2016; Rühlemann & Gries, 2020, 2021; Tantucci & Wang, 2018, 2021, 2022; Van Olmen & Tantucci, 2022). We contribute to this line of research by using different types of regression models including generalised linear models and random forests. The models are at varying levels of complexity, ranging from simpler models with one independent variable and a binary dependent outcome to more complex models with several independent variables and multiple levels of outcome. The goal is to show the potential of the models to answer different questions in pragmatics. In some places, we have chosen a model with fewer predictors over a model with more predictors in order to ease the reader into multifactorial corpus pragmatic analyses and to keep the level of statistical complexity manageable to novices. We used the software environment RStudio (version 1.3.1093; RStudio Team, 2020) for all analyses.

To compare the occurrences of the advice constructions first across LLC–1 and LLC–2 and then across casual and institutional conversation, we fitted a number of binary logistic regression models to our data using the *glm* function of the *stats* package in base R. An advantage of regression models over traditional monofactorial tests (e.g., chi-squared tests) is that all the levels of the independent variable, that is, the advice constructions, are considered together. The plots comparing the occurrence of the constructions across the corpora and the conversational contexts were generated using the *ggplot2* package. To predict the outcome of advice based on the range of linguistic, dialogic, and social factors, we modelled the data using Conditional Random Forests (CRFs), implemented in the *cforest* function of the *party* package (Strobl *et al.*, 2008). CRFs have been widely used in syntactic analyses of language to predict particular linguistic variants (e.g., Klavan *et al.*, 2015; Larsson *et al.*, 2020; Szmrecsanyi *et al.*, 2016; Tagliamonte & Baayen, 2012); however, they have not been used very often in corpus pragmatics (but see Tantucci & Wang, 2018, 2022; Van Olmen & Tantucci, 2022) despite the fact that CRFs are particularly useful in situations with highly correlated predictors, and where the sample size is small but the number of predictors is large – a common scenario in pragmatics research, and also the case in the present study. CRFs are based on Conditional Inference Trees (function: *ctree*), which predict outcomes by recursively partitioning the data into smaller and smaller branches and leaves according to those predictors that co-vary most strongly with the outcome.[13] CRFs extend that by using 'ensemble methods in a forest of trees built on randomly sampled data subsets to arrive at an aggregated estimate of a particular outcome's probability' (Szmrecsanyi *et al.*, 2016:114), and they also rank the predictors based on their explanatory importance. In the final model, we grew 1,000 trees (*ntree* = 1000) and selected three random predictors for each tree (*mtry* = 3; square root of the total number of predictors; see

---

[13] For introductions to CRFs and CITs, see Levshina (2015, 2021) and Gries (2019).

Levshina, 2015:297). As before, we used the *ggplot2* package to visualise the proportions of the levels of the most important predictors.

As previously mentioned, the output of the statistical models was intended as a basis for further qualitative analysis. Also, due to data sparseness we were not able to include all levels of all the factors in the statistical models, requiring some simplification. However, the fine-grained analysis proposed in this section provided us with useful entry points for further qualitative investigations of specific advice situations. The next section presents the results of the qualitative and quantitative approaches.

4 Results and Discussion

This section is divided into two parts, focusing on the adviser and the advisee, respectively. Section 4.1 takes the perspective of the adviser and examines the linguistic constructions used to give advice in natural spontaneous conversation, while Section 4.2 takes the perspective of the advisee and their reactions to the advice with respect to constructional choice as well as the dialogic and social factors of the advice sequences.

4.1 Advice-Giving in Conversation

For the analysis of the advisers' contributions, we analysed 1,234 advice-giving utterances from LLC. Of these, 63 per cent (775 occurrences) are from LLC–2 and 37 per cent (459 occurrences) are from LLC–1. Among the two types of conversation included in the study, conversations between equals and disparates, there are more instances of advice given among people who have hierarchically different positions. Normalised to frequencies per 10,000 words, conversations between disparates include forty-nine advice-giving utterances, while conversations between equals include nineteen. These preliminary observations offer a good estimation of the overall patterns in the data; however, the diversity of the linguistic forms of the advice-giving utterances requires a more systematic approach to the types of constructions and how they vary across time and discourse contexts. Section 4.1.1 proposes a classification of the advice constructions, and Section 4.1.2 puts this classification to use by comparing the frequencies of the construction types across LLC–1 and LLC–2, and casual and institutional conversation.

4.1.1 Classification of Advice Constructions

In this section, we start by proposing a classification of the constructions used to give advice in LLC relative to their degree of speaker authority, and we then relate the types of constructions to the degree of communicative (in)directness and face considerations. As previously mentioned, the development of the classification of the advice constructions was based on three linguistic factors: (i) the form of advice, (ii) utterance type, and (iii) the presence or absence of modifiers. These factors were manually examined and correlations between them were identified for the classification of the types of unsubstantiated as well as substantiated constructions that speakers of English draw on in advice frames. Our classification was aided by previous work on advice constructions, which has proposed similar classifications, albeit only partial ones in terms of the range of the constructions (see below). It follows that the classification is not strictly data driven but rather the result of subjective, yet explicit, decisions made by the annotators with support from existing research. On the basis of the three factors, we classified all 1,234 utterances in the sample relative to their degree of speaker authority. The notion of speaker authority was operationalised in terms of the degree of the deontic force of the advice, and the strength of epistemic commitment and confidence conveyed by the speaker or adviser. The constructions form a continuum ranging from constructions that are expressive of the strongest degree of deontic force coupled with the highest level of the speaker's epistemic commitment and confidence about the benefits of the advice for the advisee at the one end, to constructions that are only weakly deontic with low speaker commitment and confidence at the other end. The order of the continuum of constructions follows from our analysis of the constructions in their various contexts in the dialogic sequences. We then consider the speaker authority continuum with reference to the notion of communicative (in)directness, which also forms a continuum that to some extent goes hand in hand with the degree of speaker authority. The concurrence is likely to be a natural consequence of the fact that speakers' choice of (in)direct expressions is a matter that relates to their intersubjective social and psychological considerations of the advisee. The choice of form is utilised by advisers to make it easier or more difficult to express alternatives, that is, to expand or contract the communicative space vis-à-vis the advisee (cf. Section 1.1).

Table 8 shows the types of constructions and their instantiations in LLC, ordered in terms of strength of speaker authority. The left-most column features five general-level types of constructions and their subtypes; we refer to them as unsubstantiated as they are not substantiated by language forms. The introduction of subtypes allows us to make comparisons at different levels of constructional granularity across the corpora and the discourse contexts (see Section 4.1.2). The column in the middle displays representative substantiated examples of the constructions from the corpora. The most important parts of the examples are underlined. Absence of constructions in Table 8 does not mean that such constructions cannot be used to give advice, but it simply means that

Table 8 The constructions and their instantiations in LLC, ordered on a continuum of deontic and epistemic speaker authority (Strong = strongly directive, committed, confident; Weak = weakly directive, committed, confident); the most important parts of the examples are underlined

Constructions		Examples	Speaker authority
			Strong
Imperatives	Affirmative/negative	well *don't do that*	
	Exhortative	*let's begin with* your own department	
Performatives	Verb	I would strongly *suggest* that you add on some contingency	
	Noun	well my *advice* would be to try *Nuffield*	
Interrogatives	Negated: Mixed reference	why *don't you just send her a text* *couldn't we discuss fundraising* *would it not be possible to shift the library to the block across*	
	Non-negated: Reference to advisee	*have you ever looked in other parts of the library* *would you like to take some lunch*	
	Non-negated: Reference to both	what if *we just used loads of scaredy's stuff* *can we reply and say we had a vote*	
	Non-negated: Reference to action	what about *double glazing* *could it be in the tutorial hour*	
Declaratives	Necessity: Reference to advisee	*you mustn't think of it as fiddling* *you need to get some Norse friends* *I don't think you should feel coerced into doing anything*	
	Necessity: Reference to both	I think that *we mustn't worry too much about this* that's what *we need to wear* *we shouldn't typecast people*	
	Necessity/possibility: Reference to adviser	*I should continue also to give Professor Pitt's* *I wouldn't feel sorry for him*	
	Possibility: Reference to advisee	structure is something *you can always talk about* *you could investigate*	**Weak**

Strong ←——————→ Weak

Possibility: Reference to both — *maybe we can go to your mum's that week*
we might jolly well use them

Necessity/possibility: Reference to action — *there ought to be a textbook*
it would be great to kind of push it down the line

Fragment — *maybe just after the end of the term*

Complete — *well if you just write to Paxted College you'll get him*

Insubordinate — *if you feel like a film tomorrow night Mike*

Conditionals

no examples were found in our data. The column to the right presents the ordering of the constructions as a function of the degree of speaker authority as well as the extent to which we assume the advisee is expected to follow the advice. The ordering applies both to the general-level constructions and the specific examples of the constructions in the middle column. As shown in Table 8, the principal order of speaker authority is: imperatives → performatives → interrogatives → declaratives → conditionals. This order partly mirrors Couper-Kuhlen's and Thompson's (2022) order – imperatives → interrogatives → declaratives – but it also differs from theirs since they did not consider performatives and conditionals, at least not as separate categories.

The investigation of the occurrence of the different constructions in LLC shows that utterances in the imperative mood, the highest level of the continuum, make up 22 per cent of all the advice-giving utterances in the sample (276/1,234). They represent the most straightforward way of trying to make somebody else do something for their own benefit. Giving advice in the imperative puts clear constraints on the advisee's uptake in most situations – an uptake of acceptance (or not) is expected by the adviser. In affirmations, such utterances convey an obligation, and in negated form, a prohibition (*don't do that*), which do not leave much room for debate or negotiation. The exhortative *let's* utterance is a special and a slightly softer type of imperative construction and less binding from the advisee's point of view since it includes the adviser and conveys a piece of advice where the interlocutors share part of the burden. In our data, both types of imperatives are often modified by hedges (26 per cent of the time), but rarely by emphasisers (5 per cent), which speaks to their forcefulness and need for softening.

Next on the continuum of speaker authority in Table 8 are performatives, which make up a very small part of the sample (1 per cent or 12/1,234). They are expressions that explicitly state that an act of advice-giving is being performed. The performative expressions may be verbs (*I would strongly suggest that . . .*) or nouns (*well my advice would be to . . .*), with verbs coming across as more forceful. Unlike directives in the imperative, mention of the advisee is optional in performatives, softening the impact of the advice on the recipient; the advisers, on the other hand, are always explicitly identified, adding personal involvement and highlighting the higher authority assumed by the adviser. Due to the limited number of performatives in the sample, we cannot say much about patterns of modification. However, as the examples in Table 8 indicate, performatives can be modified by both hedges and emphasisers.

Next in terms of deontic force and epistemic commitment and confidence are different types of interrogatives, which occur in the sample 7 per cent of the time (82/1,234). They necessarily appeal directly to the advisee, from whom a response is expected. We consider negated interrogatives to be more deontically forceful and epistemically committed than non-negated interrogatives, regardless of whether reference is given to the advisee, both the advisee and the adviser, or to the action instead. This is because only negated interrogatives convey that 'the solution being recommended is so obvious or natural that there must be good reason *not* to embrace it' (Couper-Kuhlen & Thompson, 2022). Among both the negated and non-negated interrogatives, the more forceful are constructions with an explicit mention of the advisee followed by an explicit mention of both parties, in which case the burden of the action is shared. Utterances without any mention of the participants but with reference to action instead are the least compelling ones, because the information about who should carry out the action is held back. The negated and non-negated interrogatives also have in common that questions introduced by, for example, *wh-*words (*why don't you*/*what about*) are stronger than their modal counterparts expressing possibility (*would it not*/*could it*). This is because the former are more explicit in their call for action. Interestingly, in our data only a small proportion of all the interrogatives (21 per cent) are modified in one way or another, and if they are, they are typically hedged. The negated interrogatives are more likely to be hedged than their non-negated counterparts, presumably due to their strength. We consider interrogatives to rank higher on the continuum of speaker authority than the next category, namely, declaratives, because the former are more explicit in their demand for an answer and so are more impositive. Leech makes a note about the relative strength of interrogatives and declaratives in requests, which we believe applies to advice as well.

> [T]o avoid impoliteness, *O* [other] is virtually obliged to make some kind of answer, whereas in the declarative pattern a noncommittal reply, or even no reply, is more tolerable. A negative answer to the question–a refusal–is in some degree impolite ... and so *O* may feel constrained to say *Yes*. (Leech, 2014:152–153)

Next on the continuum of speaker authority are declaratives, which are the most frequent type of construction in the sample (65 per cent or 806/1,234). As shown in Table 8, they come in several different flavours, ranging from more forceful formats of advice as conveyed by modal auxiliaries of necessity to less forceful formats with modal auxiliaries of possibility. The necessity modals are exemplified by stronger core modals (*must*), various types of semi-modals (*have to, need to, want to*), and weaker core modals (*should*), in that order, and the possibility modals by *can* (stronger), and *could, might,* and *would* (weaker). The order of declaratives in Table 8 partly mirrors Couper-Kuhlen's and Thompson's (2022) order – *you should/ought to* → *I'd/I would/I wouldn't* → *you can/could* – however, they remain agnostic about mixed constructions of necessity and possibility without explicit mention of the participants (*there ought to be a textbook, it would be great to kind of push it down the line*), as well as short fragments (*maybe just after the end of the term*). Both are placed on the lowest end of the continuum in Table 8 because they leave open the source of the advice as well as who is expected to carry out the action. As with interrogatives, explicit mention of the advisee in declaratives is considered more forceful than explicit mention of both parties. Other features that may make a difference are the polarity of the modal auxiliaries, different clause patterns, and the presence or absence of contractions, but as indicated in Table 8, this is a level of detail that we are not concerned with here. Advice in declarative form combines with the most diverse range of modifiers of all the construction types. Hedges are the most common (43 per cent), but other stance markers such as *honestly* and *actually* are also used with higher frequency than in other constructions (5 per cent). Interestingly, in our sample we did not find any instances of fragments modified by emphasisers, which supports their interpretation as the least forceful type of declarative construction due to their brevity and undemanding tone. As previously mentioned, we consider declaratives to be less impositive than interrogatives due to their lack of demand for an answer. However, we acknowledge the possible overlap between the more forceful types of declaratives (e.g., necessity modals with reference to the advisee) and the less forceful interrogatives (e.g., non-negated interrogatives with reference to the action), which needs to be taken into account in quantitative analyses based on the finer-grained classification.

At the lowest level of deontic force and epistemic commitment and confidence in Table 8 are conditionals, making up 5 per cent of the sample (58/ 1,234). They are divided into two types: complete and insubordinate. In terms of strength, the stronger ones are complete conditionals with both the matrix clause and the subordinate clause expressing a predicted outcome or a hypothetical situation. Insubordinate conditionals are independent conditional clauses where the resulting outcome, given the condition, is unexpressed. They are the least forceful constructions and come with weak speaker authority. Added to this, nearly half of all the conditionals in our data (48 per cent) are modified, typically by hedges and rarely by emphasisers, thus mirroring the pattern for fragments above. As was the case with constructions at the juncture of interrogatives and declaratives, conditionals may also overlap with weaker forms of declaratives in terms of directive strength (e.g., fragments). Therefore, the finer-grained classification might be a more useful reflection of the scale of directive strength than the general-level classification (see Section 4.1.2).

To some extent parallel to the scale of speaker/adviser authority is the scale of communicative (in)directness, which concerns advisers' openness towards the advisee to alternative options and viewpoints. This scale is however not a simple reflex, or one-to-one match, of the modality scale of deontic and epistemic strength of speaker authority but overlaps with it at the top and bottom of the continuum. Unlike speaker authority, the scale of (in)directness is not primarily about deontic force and speaker commitment and confidence, but instead pertains to the intersubjective relationship and face concerns between the participants. In slightly different terms, we may say that (in)directness is at the juncture between the discursive strategies and the social and psychological processes related to the intersubjective relationship between the participants (cf. Section 1.1). As described in Section 2.3.1, damage to both the adviser's and the advisee's face are clearly at stake in situations where advice is given.

With respect to communicative (in)directness, imperatives are emblematic examples of the top of the scale. They are the most direct utterances that express advice directly and bald-on-record to the advisee. Also, at the strong end of the scale we find utterances that explicitly mention *you* as is the case with some performatives (*I would strongly suggest that you* . . .), the stronger examples of interrogatives (*why don't you* . . .), and the stronger examples of declaratives (*you must/need to/should*). In these cases, the advisee is expected to take a stand for or against the piece of advice. This contrasts with conditionals or more indirect declaratives referring to situations and entities, where the absence of a response would not be strange. In communicatively direct utterances, the staging is simple in that the act of advice takes place in the actual speech situation as a bald-on-record directive message from the adviser to the advisee, and the latter can accept or resist the piece of advice by saying *yes* or *no*. In such cases, potential harm to the interlocutors' face derives primarily from the unambiguous advisory nature of the utterances. The adviser cannot plausibly claim deniability, should the advice be unwelcome, and the advisee has fewer (linguistic and practical) opportunities to avoid engaging with the advice, thus risking damage to their own as well as the adviser's self-image.

Now, indirectness may already come into the picture in these sequences in the form of various kinds of hedging strategies since it concerns the portrayal of a piece of advice where the speaker sets up an alternative mental space in order to move away from the here and now to a space that recognises that the advisee may have different thoughts about the situation (e.g., *what about, I would, you can*; Fauconnier, 1994). This is an important strategy of intersubjective consideration of face to promote successful mutual coordination of mental states in communication. With respect to indirectness in the communicative sense of the term that we use here, speakers link the here-and-now space with an irrealis space (Paradis, 2009, 2020), which in turn has the effect of expanding the workspace of the common ground for the uptake/perlocution. By using alternative mental spaces, the adviser also saves their own face. As previously observed, the adviser's self-esteem is at risk if the advisee is unwilling to accept the advice. The alternative mental space has the effect of playing down the level of epistemic control on the part of the adviser and encourages the advisee to assess other options (cf. Couper-Kuhlen & Thompson, 2022). Therefore, by giving the advisee a way to feel included in the process, advisers boost the advisee's face at the same time as they reduce the damage to their own face in the case the advice is turned down.

The above types of indirectness are all spatial construals that have a mitigating effect on the intersubjective bonding between the adviser and the advisee. They portray the piece of advice in a more modest and considerate way than the strongly assertive direct forms where the speaker's viewpoint is *the* non-debatable viewpoint. Such space builders establish mental spaces that are distinct from the reality space of the communicative situation. In the case of imperatives and deontic modal utterances with expressions such as *you must/ need to/should*, the advisee has the option of accepting or rejecting the advice by saying *yes* or *no*, while in the case of speakers' portrayal of the advice in a communicatively indirect way, the advisee is treated with intersubjective consideration as a thoughtful person that is capable of assessing a piece of advice and its consequences. In other words, directness in our sense has the effect of contracting the communicative space, while indirectness has the opposite effect of expanding it (Põldvere *et al.*, 2016). A simple response in the form of a *yes* or *no* in the uptake by the advisee is infelicitous in the case of advice presented in the indirect way. Some kind of elaboration on the part of the advisee is expected in such sequences.

4.1.2 Comparison of the Constructions across Corpora and Contexts

In this section, we compare the frequencies of the types of advice constructions in Table 8 across LLC–1 and LLC–2 and the conversational contexts, between equals and disparates, which by and large correspond to casual and institutional conversation. The goal is to track the development of the constructions over the past fifty years in spoken British English with respect to the degree of deontic and epistemic speaker authority as well as communicative (in)directness and the interlocutors' intersubjective consideration of each other's face concerns. The same principle will be applied to the conversational contexts, where the goal is to determine the role of context in constructional choice and thereby to complement existing conversation analytic investigations of advice with a more comprehensive understanding of how, if at all, advice-giving differs across casual and institutional contexts and among different constellations of people. We start with the diachronic investigation.

As previously mentioned, there are many more instances of advice in the sample from LLC–2 than LLC–1 (775 and 459 occurrences, respectively). While this difference is interesting, we refrain from drawing any conclusions as to the reason for the more frequent use of advice-giving in contemporary conversation compared to fifty years ago. Instead, we are interested in the constructions used in each period. The corpora follow the same pattern in terms of the proportions of the general-level constructions in Table 8 (imperatives, performatives, interrogatives, declaratives, conditionals). This is illustrated in Figure 2, which shows that the most common way to give advice in both LLC–1 and LLC–2 is through declaratives, followed by imperatives, interrogatives, conditionals, and performatives, in that order. However, the corpora differ from each other in terms of the more frequent use of imperatives and declaratives in LLC–2 compared to LLC–1, and the less frequent use of all other forms of advice-giving. Specifically, the regression model identified a significant association between LLC–2 and imperatives ($\beta = 0.8438$, $SE = 0.1313$, $z = 6.429$, $p < 0.001$), and between LLC–1 and interrogatives ($\beta = -0.8438$, $SE = 0.2569$, $z = -3.284$, $p = 0.001$), and conditionals ($\beta = -0.9820$, $SE = 0.2942$, $z = -3.338$, $p < 0.001$).[14] Declaratives did not reach significance ($\beta = -0.2945$, $SE = 0.1503$, $z = -1.960$, $p = 0.05$), and we excluded performatives due to their low number in the data.[15] In Table 8, we placed interrogatives and conditionals at opposite ends of the scale of directive strength, with imperatives at the very top. Therefore, these findings call for a closer investigation of what might be behind the seemingly contradictory results. On the one hand, it seems clear that the more recent dataset includes more imperatives and fewer conditionals; on the other hand, the older dataset also comprises some of the strongly directive, and unambiguously advice-giving, interrogatives. In other words, the shift towards more democratic and less deontic forms of advice that we hypothesised based on previous research appears not to have materialised.

---

[14] All the regression models in this section are given in the supplementary material of the Element.

[15] It should be noted that, during the annotation phase, we noticed an unusually high number of imperatives in one text in LLC–2 in particular (a study abroad advisory session). The present regression models do not take into account the random variation introduced by the peculiarities of particular conversations, as mixed-effects models would do (see Gries, 2015b). The reason for not using mixed-effects models in this Element is because a model with fixed effects was considered to be more appropriate for a dataset with a high number of random effects and a comparatively low number of actual observations. However, even after we had removed the above-mentioned text from the analysis, the regression model maintained a significant association between LLC–2 and imperatives, as well as between LLC–1 and the other construction types. Therefore, we are confident that the results are not affected by the peculiarities of one text, but that they reflect the whole dataset (but see Seitanidi *et al.*, forthcoming for a critical assessment of the comparability between LLC–1 and LLC–2).

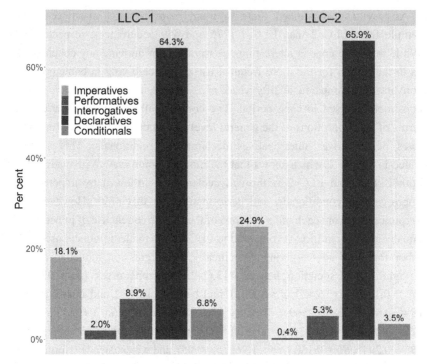

Figure 2 Comparison of general-level advice constructions across LLC–1 and LLC–2

A more nuanced picture emerges when we consider the finer-grained constructions in Table 8. Some constructions were conflated due to low numbers, resulting in eight different types of constructions: affirmative/negative and exhortative imperatives; negated and non-negated interrogatives; declaratives expressing necessity, possibility, and declaratives with reference to the action (both mixed declaratives and fragments); and, finally, conditionals (both complete and insubordinate). The regression model revealed a significant association between LLC–2 and affirmative/negative imperatives (β = 0.8829, SE = 0.1453, z = 6.078, p < 0.001), and between LLC–1 and negated interrogatives (β = −1.4135, SE = 0.4242, z = −3.332, p < 0.001), non-negated interrogatives (β = −0.6270, SE = 0.3083, z = −2.034, p = 0.042), declaratives with reference to the action (β = −0.5569, SE = 0.1976, z = −2.819, p = 0.005), and conditionals (β = −1.0211, SE = 0.3007, z = −3.396, p < 0.001). The rest of the construction types did not reach significance (see the supplementary material for details). The results support our decision to propose the fine-grained classification of advice in Table 8, without which we would have been unable to isolate the precise differences in construction types across the corpora. Specifically, we find that, while declaratives did not reach overall significance, those with reference to the action (*it would be great to kind of push it down the line, maybe just after the end of the term*) are more common in the older data. Compared to declarative constructions that place the burden of the action on specific individuals, declaratives with reference to the action have a more ambiguous and indirect advisory nature whereby the advisee is presented as a person who is capable of making their own decision.

On the one hand, then, the decline of less forceful types of declaratives and conditionals (*if you feel like a film tomorrow night Mike*) seems to point to a move towards stronger forms of advice-giving today. Indeed, it is the stronger forms of imperatives (affirmative/negative rather than exhortative) that are more common in LLC–2 (compare *well don't do that* and *let's begin with your own department*). On the other hand, it is clear that negated interrogatives, in particular, carry a similar force to imperatives with regard to directness in conversation and their potential impact on the interlocutors' relationship. We suggest that what we are seeing over time is a change from interrogatives to imperatives in what is considered the default form for the most explicit and face-harming instances of advising. However, the rise of imperatives does not necessarily mean that advice today is overly indicative of unequal interaction. Instead, we argue that elaborate forms of advice-giving such as conditionals, despite being low on the face damage scale, can still be perceived as socially distancing due to excessive indirectness and elaborateness. They are more indicative of the kind of Victorian individualistic politeness observed by Culpeper and Demmen (2011) in the nineteenth century. Democratisation, then, is not just a question of strong or weak modality, but of a more general shift towards more informal and less elaborate and convoluted ways of giving advice, which can include more direct ones, too. From the perspective of politeness-as-conventionalisation, we consider direct forms of advising as becoming, over time, more acceptable and socially appropriate, a result which ties in with Culpeper's and Demmen's observation about the use of requests in recent decades. The social acceptance of more direct forms of advising can be fruitfully explored in other aspects of interaction, too, which leads us to differences between conversations between equals and disparates.

For comparisons between conversations between equals and disparates, we considered the whole dataset to be able to draw meaningful conclusions about the two types of conversational context. As previously mentioned, advice-giving utterances in conversations between disparates in LLC are more than twice as frequent as in conversations between equals; they contain forty-nine utterances, while conversations between equals contain nineteen utterances (per 10,000

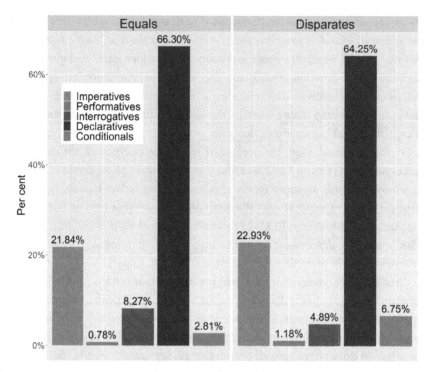

Figure 3 Comparison of general-level advice constructions across
conversations between equals and disparates

words). This is not surprising considering that, in the former, the conversations
mainly take place in institutional contexts where advice is implicitly solicited
through the roles given to the participants, while in the latter, advice is given in
casual contexts and therefore not necessarily solicited or expected. In terms of the
proportion of the general-level advice constructions in each conversational context, the results seem to mirror the patterns above, but with one major exception:
in   conversations   between   disparates,   the   third   most   common
construction type is no longer interrogatives, but conditionals (see Figure 3).
This was confirmed in the regression model, which showed a significant
association between conversations between disparates and conditionals
($\beta = 0.82750$, $SE = 0.30830$, $z = 2.684$, $p = 0.007$); for conversations between
equals, a significant association was found for interrogatives ($\beta = -0.57401$,
$SE = 0.26047$, $z = -2.204$, $p = 0.028$). No significant differences between
the conversational contexts were found for imperatives ($\beta = -0.02899$,
$SE = 0.12040$, $z = -0.241$, $p = 0.81$) or declaratives ($\beta = -0.08030$,
$SE = 0.13955$, $z = -0.575$, $p = 0.565$). Performatives were again excluded due
to low numbers. As before, the fine-grained constructions revealed a more

nuanced picture. In addition to the significant association between conversations between disparates and conditionals (β = 0.789774, *SE* = 0.313086, $z = 2.523, p = 0.012$), the regression model also revealed a significant association between conversations between equals and negated interrogatives ($\beta = -1.058556, SE = 0.458611, z = -2.308, p = 0.021$). The remaining differences were not significant (see the supplementary material).

Taken together, the results seem to support the interpretation that, in casual conversation where advice is not typically the default aim of the conversation, it is given in a way that is more recognisable to the advisee, that is, by using communicatively direct forms of the type *why don't you* (cf. Couper-Kuhlen & Thompson, 2022). Interlocutors who know each other well may also feel more comfortable giving advice in a direct way due to reduced face concerns. Constructions where the advisee is explicitly mentioned could therefore be seen as supportive moves between equals working together to address the problem immediately. This is different from conversations between disparates, which favour conditionals. The indirectness of conditionals could be perceived as unnecessarily roundabout and formal in casual conversation, but in institutional contexts where the participants typically are merely acquaintances, conditionals are useful because they soften the potential blow of the advice and draw the advisee in by opening up the space for alternative viewpoints. We observe further qualitative differences between the social settings when the conversations between disparates are broken down to show the direction of the advice-giving: to or from a person of higher status. When advice is given by a person of higher status, for example, by an employer to an employee or a supervisor to a supervisee, it seems to be more direct, particularly through the use of affirmative/negative imperatives. Such imperatives carry a high risk of damage both to the adviser's and the advisee's face as they carry the expectation of compliance from the advisee and position them as not being capable of considering alternatives, and they also position the adviser as being entitled to issue such uncontroversial advice. However, if the imperatives are of a positive kind, they could in fact enhance face by presenting the adviser as someone who cares about the interlocutor. We came across several such imperatives particularly in the LLC–2 data. Consider (22), a study abroad advisory session where adviser A's negative imperatives (italicised) are meant to encourage student B to apply for a year abroad.[16]

---

[16] In the following examples, we have retained most of the markups of the spoken texts, including pauses (<pause/>) and non-verbal vocalisations (<vocal desc="laughs"/>) in order to render a faithful account of the dynamics of the original conversations.

(22)   A: but that's it's okay *don't worry* but I would just say *don't worry don't worry*
             too much I know that's easier said than done
        B: yeah <vocal desc="laughs"/>
        A: cause you know it's just a big it's such an integral part of the next year
             but I really wouldn't worry too much … yeah oh also *don't*
             worry I can't stress that enough oh I feel really worried now that I've like
             I've made things way more complicated yeah *don't worry*

We also found other kinds of strong imperatives in the conversation, which concern the student's choice of destinations (*stick with those regions, don't go too wild card, put California first*). The adviser's viewpoint is presented as *the* viewpoint with little space for the student to participate in the problem-solving process. However, the social setting is such that the use of these imperatives is unlikely to be affected by face concerns because the adviser's knowledge and experience give her the authority to issue the advice, and in most cases the advice has also been made relevant by the advisee (e.g., *I've made myself sick [worrying] about [it]*). Moreover, this pattern seems to be more common in LLC–2 than in LLC–1. Consider the example in (23) from LLC–1, which is comparable to the examples from LLC–2; they all involve advice given by a person of higher status and are about a life-changing decision for the advisee. However, the difference is that, in (23), adviser A uses the conditional construction *if you were living in London* to guide advisee B's future action.

(23)   A: how far is it from Huddersfield to Coventry
        B: uhm about uhm a hundred miles
        A: so in fact *if you were living in London* during that period you
             would be closer

This apparent difference between the corpora supports the interpretation above, namely, that direct forms of advising have become more acceptable and socially appropriate today. However, more research is needed to unpack the changes in each social setting using more complex models, as well as with regard to changes within the construction types observed here. The fact that declaratives expressing necessity, for example, did not show any differences might be because this category is rather broad and includes necessity modals of varying strengths (compare *must* and *should*); their development may therefore be more complex than our analysis might have revealed (see Põldvere, forthcoming).

Equally important to the advice frames is the outcome of the advice or how the advisee actually responds to the advice constructions in different discourse contexts, and the interaction of these factors with other relevant aspects of advice exchanges. For instance, the fact that advice is either explicitly or implicitly solicited in conversation, as in (22)–(23), does not necessarily mean that it is well received by the advisee, so the full dialogic sequence needs to be taken into account. In the following, we expand the current investigation by identifying the full frames of advice exchanges in LLC.

4.2 Advice Uptake in Conversation

For the analysis of advice uptake, we turned to CRFs to rank the importance of the constructional, dialogic, and social factors in predicting advice outcomes in the conversations from LLC. Due to data sparseness, we conflated the levels of some of the factors in the CRF but kept the finer-grained levels for qualitative analysis. The constructions are the general-level advice constructions in Table 8. As before, we excluded performatives due to low numbers. The dialogic factors are type of event and deictic time, as well as three levels of (non-)solicitation of advice: advisee asks for advice/information/opinion, advisee discloses a problem/announces a plan of action, and adviser identifies a problem/volunteers advice. The three levels are clearly distinct in that, in the first case, the advisability of the action is explicitly or implicitly stated, while in the second case, the presence of a problem or a plan may make advice solicitation plausible. The third level comprises all instances of adviser-initiated advice, that is, when the advice is not solicited by the advisee. The social factors are the relationship between the interlocutors (equals versus disparates), and their age and gender. In the case of age, we excluded situations where the advice was directed at people of different ages (40 occurrences), and gender was simplified to a binary variable consisting of same-gender versus mixed-gender conversations. No interactions between the variables were included in the final CRF, because comparisons with models with the interactions did not indicate any improvement. The response variable, the advisee's response to the advice, has three levels: acceptance, resistance/rejection, other response. The decision to conflate resistance and rejection was based on our initial observation of the data, where both types of advice uptake behaved in a fairly similar way, as well as the tendency for much of the previous conversation analytic research to group them under the same umbrella (e.g., Couper-Kuhlen & Thompson, 2022; Hepburn & Potter, 2011; Pudlinski, 2002). Finally, the conversations from LLC–1 and LLC–2 were combined to provide a general overview of advice outcomes in Present-Day spoken British English.

Overall, the most common types of advice uptake in our data are other responses (36 per cent; 421/1,182) and resistance or rejection (35 per cent; 410/1,182), with acceptance as the least frequent category (30 per cent; 351/1,182). This seems to hold true regardless of variation in formal and contextual

Conditional variable importance

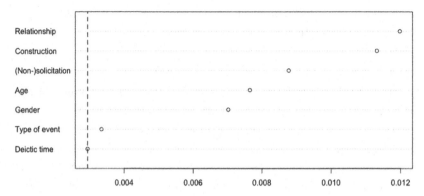

Figure 4 Conditional variable importance of a CRF of three types of advice uptake: acceptance, resistance/rejection, other response

features of the interactions. Figure 4 presents a dotchart showing the conditional variable importance of each of the predictors of advice uptake in the CRF. To assess how well the model fits the data, we computed the accuracy measure based on a prediction matrix (Levshina, 2021:22). The accuracy measure showed that the model has higher accuracy than chance, but not by much: 0.63 (see below). In Figure 4, the predictors are listed in descending order of importance, with relationship as the most important predictor with a variable importance score of 0.012, followed closely by construction (0.011), and further behind are (non-)solicitation (0.009), age (0.008), and gender (0.007).[17] Type of event has comparatively little discriminatory power (0.003), and deictic time has no discriminatory power at all. In what follows, we discuss in detail the two most important predictors of advice uptake in our data, relationship and construction, and discuss briefly the other two predictors which showed interesting differences, namely, (non-)solicitation and age.

The distribution of advice sequences in terms of the relationship between the interlocutors, or conversations between equals and disparates, shows clear differences across the types of advice uptake (see Figure 5). In particular, the distributional relationship is almost reversed for acceptance, on the one hand, and resistance or rejection, on the other, so that speakers who are on an equal footing are more likely to resist or reject the advice (40 per cent versus 29 per cent), whereas speakers who have hierarchically unequal positions are more likely to accept it (34 per cent versus 26 per cent).

---

[17] Variable importance scores quantify the size of the effect that a predictor has on the response variable (Gries, 2019:7). The cut-off point tends to be the absolute minimum value, and the rest of the values should be interpreted with regard to their ranking, without comparing the scores across different datasets (Levshina, 2015:21).

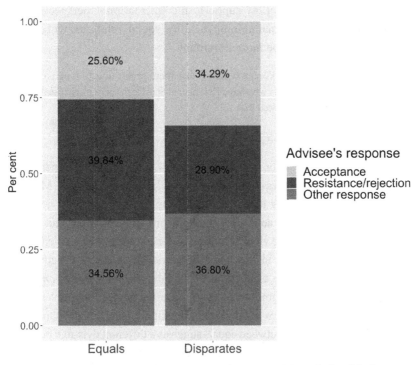

Figure 5 Distribution of advice sequences in terms of the relationship between the interlocutors across three types of advice outcomes

Surprisingly, the pattern for disparates seems to be the same in both directions: to or from a person of higher status. As for advice given by a person of higher status, the pattern aligns with our understanding of face concerns; acceptance is the preferred response to advice in the discursive frame, and especially where power relations are concerned, it may be difficult for advisees of lower status to voice their true thoughts and feelings. They would need strong reasons to resist or reject the advice and therefore potentially harm both their own self-image and that of their superior. Example (24), from a work meeting in LLC–2, illustrates this well.[18] Here, speaker A, the superior person, asks B to carry out an action to which B responds with the marked acknowledgement *yes*, a form of acceptance. However, it becomes clear after A's next utterance (*although I think you checked that*) that, in reality, B had already done what A suggested. This provides support for Jefferson's and Lee's (1981) idea of advice uptake as more or less independent of real-world action; if this were the case, B's response would have been to assert prior knowledge and/or competence (a form of resistance) with respect to the advice.

---

[18] Square brackets indicate speaker overlaps.

Instead, the exchange in (24) supports the interactional perspective on advice uptake whereby maintaining healthy social relations with one's superior is considered to be more important.

(24)   A: also if you could check please that there aren't any bits of post from
               postgrad students who have [left because] of yeah there might be although
               I think you checked that
          B: [yes]
          B: did that yeah

A possible explanation for the opposite pattern, advice given *to* a person of higher status, lies in the types of conversations included in the corpora. Many of them include brainstorming activities where employees share their views on possible courses of future action for the company or institution, and where employers take a favourable view of the ideas to encourage active participation. This is reflected in the way in which the superiors tend to accept the advice in our data; they give positive evaluations of the advice (*that's a good one/call*) rather than make clear commitments to act upon the advice themselves, as is often the case when the roles are reversed. The higher levels of resistance and rejection in conversations between equals suggests a different dynamic between people who know each other well, such as friends and family. Close relationships between interlocutors reduce the pressure to accept the advice and allow the advisee to be either forthright in their rejection or less committal, for instance, by using unmarked acknowledgements, presumably safe in the knowledge that the relationship is stable enough to withstand potential damage to face. This said, our results indicate how difficult it is to issue a directive in situations where the interlocutors have little or no institutional rights to do so, despite possible benefits for the advisee. This suggests that there is a need for a shift in researchers' focus on advice from institutional to casual conversation, where the stakes may be lower but where positive and productive outcomes for interlocutors are much harder to achieve.

The next predictor of importance for advice uptake in the CRF is constructional choice. As shown in Figure 6, the patterns that stand out most are: (i) the high levels of resistance or rejection observed for conditionals (44 per cent) and interrogatives (43 per cent), and (ii) the tendency for imperatives to be met with responses other than (non-)acceptance of advice (47 per cent). The results for interrogatives align with Couper-Kuhlen's and Thompson's (2022) findings that deontically stronger advice-giving formats such as the interrogative *why don't you* are often met with resistance or rejection. However, conditionals, which are deontically weaker formats, do not show clear opposite trends, despite being somewhat more likely to lead to acceptance than the other construction types in

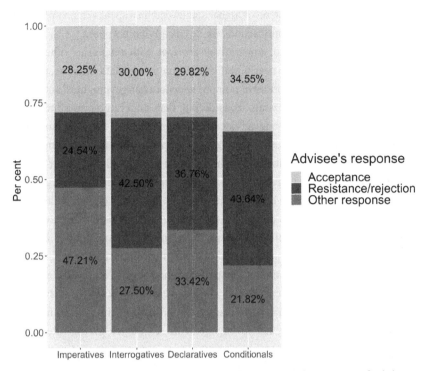

Figure 6 Distribution of advice constructions across three types of advice outcomes

our data. We interpret this apparent paradox as having to do with the ambiguous advisory nature of conditionals, which allows the interlocutors to exploit the meaning potential of the construction for their specific communicative purposes. On the one hand, then, advisees may show appreciation for the advisers' invitation to take a collaborative approach to problem-solving by accepting or at least agreeing with the adviser that a piece of advice is informative and helpful (cf. Couper-Kuhlen & Thompson, 2022). On the other hand, though, the implicit nature of conditionals may give advisees more freedom to curtail such advice-giving moves through higher levels of resistance or rejection (cf. Shaw *et al.*, 2015). It is therefore not surprising that the advice given by speaker A in (23) in Section 4.1.2 was met with an elaborated rejection by B in the subsequent turn, explaining her reasons for not being able to move to London: *uhm yes but really I mean I ought to be at home because I've got to arrange everything for the wedding.* However, despite the negative outcome of the exchange, neither of the interlocutor's faces are particularly at risk; in fact, the adviser has boosted the advisee's face by including her in the problem-solving process while reducing damage to his own face. This also eases the pressure on

B to accept advice from a person of higher status, and thus speaks in favour of the usefulness of conditional constructions for advice-giving purposes.

As previously mentioned, imperatives are met with responses other than (non-)acceptance of advice nearly half of the time in our data. Such responses include silence at the next possible point of speaker change, laughter, and topic shifts. This result is surprising, considering that imperatives are the most straightforward way of giving advice and that an uptake of acceptance (or not) is expected by the advisee, who has few opportunities to avoid engaging with the advice without damaging both their own and the adviser's self-image (cf. Section 4.1.1). We suggest that it is exactly this lack of manoeuvring space that forces advisees to find other alternatives, opting to not engage at all with advice they do not wish to accept as it is less harmful to face than having to explicitly reject or not commit to it. Also, imperatives tend to be rather short in form and so advisers might pack several of them into a single turn. The fast pace of natural conversation means that a response to each one of them by the advisee might not be desirable. For example, it would have been awkward or strange for speaker B in (22) in Section 4.1.2 to insert a response every time A told him not to worry; instead, B chose not to engage with A's advice-giving utterances immediately but to launch a more substantial turn later in the conversation.

Finally, we turn to the distributions of (non-)solicitation and age. In the former, we observe a higher level of resistance or rejection in situations where the advisee has disclosed a problem or announced a plan of action. A closer look at the data revealed that this pattern applies more clearly to troubles-telling among equals. This is illustrated in (25), a conversation between romantic partners in LLC–2, who are talking about a third person and speaker A's interactions with him.[19] Despite A's troubles-telling in the prior turn (*he's literally not even asked*), B's advice (*I think you should say now . . .*) to confront this third person about his lack of involvement in A's life is still rejected (*I can't even go there because . . .*; cf. Jefferson & Lee, 1981). Examples such as this one are further indications of the challenging nature of advising in casual conversation, and the need for continued research in this area.

(25)   A: he still doesn't even know that my nan died <pause/> cause he's literally [1]
              [not even asked]
         B: [1][does he not have you] not even [2][told him]
         A: [2][he's not] he's not asked <pause/> and all the conversations we've had
              since then I've initiated <pause/> I've thrown him so many bones like he's
              got a [3][fucking graveyard <vocal desc="laughs"/>]

---

[19] Multiple overlaps have been matched by numbers.

B: [3][I think you should say now like are you] literally not even gonna ask how I am

A: <vocal desc="laughs"/> I can't even go there because like it's just gonna feed into his self-pity and bullshit

The social factor of age is only moderately responsible for predicting the advice outcomes in our data; however, one pattern, in particular, caught our attention in the Conditional Inference Trees (CITs) that we ran in addition to the CRF. Specifically, the trees revealed a significant association between imperatives used by people of different ages, on the one hand, and advice uptake, on the other, so that when the imperatives were used by younger speakers to address older ones, the uptake was almost always a resistance or a rejection. The pattern for when the adviser was older or when the speakers were roughly the same age was more similar to the overall pattern for imperatives above. This suggests an interesting power dynamic: giving unequivocal advice to somebody with more life experience could be perceived as failing to consider their learned experiences.[20]

From the outset, it has been clear that there is no single polite way to give advice, and that what is considered polite depends on the socio-cognitive frame which envelopes the whole advice event in a particular communicative situation. Even in a large dataset such as ours, there is quite a lot of variability with regard to the relationship between constructional and contextual factors, on the one hand, and the types of advice uptake, on the other, making it difficult for us to say with certainty what constitutes successful advice outcomes. We assume that this is largely due to the complex and dynamic nature of advising, which gives rise to diverse frames of advice exchanges with different outcomes. It is therefore possible that there are other factors that may have played a role, such as the dynamic unfolding of the advice sequences over time. Such factors may explain the relatively low accuracy measure obtained for the CRF; however, being able to quantify the effects of a range of constructional, dialogic, and social predictors of advice uptake in this study is a good first step towards a better understanding of the phenomenon. Also, by focusing on the frequency of people's direct experience of actual constructions in specific contexts (Terkourafi, 2005), we have avoided the pitfall of imposing our own ideas of what is polite on the interactions, and instead taken seriously the participants' expectations in each frame. Due to reduced face concerns in conversations between equals, it is possible that advice resistance is expected in such

---

[20] Since CITs are based on single trees, that is, 'only a sample of candidate predictors is randomly drawn for each individual CIT' (Levshina, 2021:6), they are not as reliable as CRFs (Gries, 2019). Thus, the result should be interpreted with that in mind.

situations, or that it is acceptable to avoid engaging with strongly worded advice for face-management purposes. Thus, politeness-as-conventionalisation has allowed us to view the social action of advice as a complex manoeuvring of conversational expectations, marking a fruitful encounter of large-scale politeness theory, Conversation Analysis, and corpus pragmatics.

5 Theoretical and Methodological Implications

Through a detailed investigation of advice, this Element proposes a new paradigm for the study of the multifaceted nature of speech acts in real communication by means of spoken corpora. This approach to corpus pragmatics, and in our case diachronic corpus pragmatics, points to the usefulness of a combination of a multi-models, mixed-methods approach to the complexities of advice-giving and advice uptake in natural conversation. We return now to our theoretical grounding and methodological choices, and summarise how they contribute to the description and explanation of directive-commissive advice acts in contemporary spoken dialogue, and also as compared to half a century ago.

Theoretically, the Element has benefitted from the combination of insights from Speech Act Theory, a usage-based, socio-cognitive approach to meaning-making in discourse, and frame-based politeness theory. Speech Act Theory is a natural starting point for pragmatics research with its general classification of utterance types based on their illocutionary function. However, as a framework for how people make use of language in real utterances in real communication, Speech Act Theory has several limitations (cf. Section 2.1). In this Element, we have both expanded the account and gone into more detail by operationalising advice as a network of instantiations of directive–commissive speech acts. We have also made sure to take meaning-making in real communication seriously through our usage-based, socio-cognitive approach, which encompasses and permeates all aspects of advice acts (cf. Figure 1 in Section 1.1).

An important feature of the socio-cognitive approach to meaning-making is the foundational premises that it rests on, namely, that meaning-making in language is dynamic, and that meaning-making and meaning negotiation in conversation are joint activities for which the establishment of a common ground is crucial for successful outcomes. Meanings and viewpoints are shared very quickly and flexibly in dialogic contexts. These characteristics entail a good deal of multi-tasking of the language resources. It is neither the case that words or larger chunks of language are atoms with fixed meaning mappings onto entities, states, and activities in a stable manner, nor that the relationship between forms and illocutionary force is fixed; instead, the meanings of words and utterances are dynamic and sensitive to contextual demands (Paradis,

2015). As shown in Section 4.1, the constructions used to give advice in English are very diverse and make different affordances for the working space in the communicative event (both by expanding and contracting it), as evidenced in the classification of the advice constructions in Table 8. It is also shown that there are significant differences in the frequency of the constructions across LLC–1 and LLC–2, and the two types of conversational contexts (equals versus disparates) in Present-Day spoken British English. This lends some validity to the robustness of the construction types in the classification, particularly the finer-grained ones. However, to be able to make absolute claims about the validity of the degree of directive strength expressed by each construction type, future work needs to provide a multidimensional classification where features such as utterance type and explicit/implicit mention of the participants are brought together in a unified way. The empirical focus of frame-based politeness theory and its view of politeness-as-conventionalisation, which nicely dovetails with our general socio-cognitive approach to meaning-making, gave us a solid theoretical foundation to interpret the quantitative interactional differences in terms of people's understanding of what is (and is not) polite across different situations, contexts, and times (but see below).

Another important feature of the socio-cognitive approach is its capacity to go beyond the specific advice constructions and take the whole discursive frame shared by the interlocutors into account. In the case of advice sequences, this entails that at least two socio-cognitive frames converge to construct a common ground of shared interests, intentions, and values in the negotiation of meanings among advisers and advisees. We showed in Section 4.2 that advice-giving and advice uptake inform each other in important ways, with certain aspects of the advice situation being strong predictors of how the advice will ultimately be received by the advisee. Considering that advice is a sensitive undertaking, with potential negative outcomes for the relationship between the interlocutors, the discursive frames and strategies are indicative of the constant interactional and intersubjective work that speakers have to do in order to maintain healthy social relations with each other. In accordance with this, we showed that the dialogic act of advice is not restricted to the two-part sequence of giving and taking, but instead is contingent on a larger discursive frame which also includes advice solicitation, whereby the subsequent uptake/perlocution of the advice is at least partly dependent on whether the advice has been explicitly solicited or not. This is in line with Haugh's (2017) three-part sequential architecture of prompting offers of assistance, which includes prompting as the first move of the communicative sequence (cf. Arundale, 2010). As in prompts for offers of assistance, the presence of a trouble in communication does not necessarily mean that the trouble constitutes an advisable element that the adviser can exploit, but instead successful advice outcomes seem to be the result of careful consideration of the whole socio-cognitive frame of the advice act. This suggests an interesting intersection between Conversation Analysis and politeness-as-conventionalisation: politeness is not just about the specific content of the utterances, but also about knowing what is expected by each speaker at a given point of the conversation. However, the dynamic and interactive nature of advice exchanges has constituted somewhat of a challenge for the establishment of clear definitions of the entire range of advice frames in this Element; thus, future work needs to use additional methods to evaluate the extent to which speech act frames are perceived as conventionalised by the interlocutors in real communication and how this affects their perceptions of politeness (see below).

The insights already gained about advice here would not have been possible without the combination of the methodological approaches we used. Our methodologically expansive take on corpus pragmatics involved qualitative, conversation analytic, and quantitative procedures with a focus on advanced multifactorial statistical analyses. While the combination of qualitative and quantitative approaches, or the use of statistical techniques, is by no means new in corpus pragmatics, the approach proposed here releases their more wide-ranging potential for pragmatics research. Stretching the boundaries of corpus pragmatics in two different directions (qualitative and statistical) may seem contradictory at first, but there are in fact synergy effects in how the two approaches can usefully complement each other. For one thing, the qualitative approach puts greater emphasis than many existing corpus pragmatic studies on the consideration of the whole discursive frame, which in our case involves a close analysis of how the advice is initiated, constructed, and received by the interlocutors. Such a dialogic view of spoken interaction is the norm in Conversation Analysis, but not so much in pragmatics where the early focus on the utterance still has a strong influence on the field. Also, through the meticulous coding procedures, a multitude of scenarios of conversational interaction were considered for each component of the advice frame, thus mirroring the level of detail in Conversation Analysis. For (non-)solicitation of advice, for example, we considered the whole range of more or less explicitly solicited advice, in addition to the more robust three-way classification. While only the latter could be considered in the statistical model, the detailed annotation in the former provided useful entry points for further qualitative analysis. Considering that the investigation started with a manual identification of the advice-giving utterances, close reading of the conversations became relevant at every stage of the analysis: beginning, middle, and end.

By using advanced multifactorial statistical analyses, we were able to explore and confirm complex associations between the range of factors relevant for advice exchanges. In corpus pragmatics so far, the interpretation of such data has often relied on the qualitative inspection of patterns from large amounts of linguistic material to understand their implications and possible causes. Multifactorial statistics, however, offers further processing aid to the linguist by highlighting, in a largely unbiased way, the most likely associations among several factors, or several levels of the factors, at once. This is also perhaps a more realistic reflection of how humans actually interact – consciously and unconsciously weaving together a web of constructional, diachronic, and sociocultural considerations in one fell swoop. There has been an explosion of statistical modelling in other areas of linguistic enquiry, such as in the study of syntactic alternations, and we believe that corpus pragmatics should keep step with these developments. The Element illustrated the use of different types of regression models at varying levels of complexity to demonstrate their potential to answer different questions about pragmatic phenomena. We would particularly like to point out the use of CRFs in this study. With few exceptions (cf. Section 3.3.3), CRFs have not been used very much in corpus pragmatics, but the idea on which they are founded (a large number of highly correlated predictors, small sample sizes) makes them particularly suitable for it. There is, however, currently no satisfactory way to deal with the random variation introduced by the peculiarities of particular conversations in CRFs, that is, random effects (Levshina, 2021:27; but see Rautionaho & Hundt, 2021 for an approach which combines the recursive partitioning of a tree-based method with generalised linear mixed models). The use of mixed-effects models, in general, is tricky in datasets with a high number of random effects and a comparatively low number of actual observations, which is often the case in pragmatics research due to the fact that manual annotation is burdensome and time-consuming. The purpose of this Element has been to introduce some of the most widely used statistical techniques to the corpus pragmatics community while at the same time keeping the level of complexity manageable, but the work must continue to find the best fit between statistical models and datasets with pragmatic analyses.

There are two more directions in which this approach to corpus pragmatics can evolve, but which were not considered here. They are (i) the combination of corpus and experimental methods, and (ii) multimodal cues of speech act solicitation and uptake. We believe that advice, or indeed any other speech act, is best studied in its natural environment because labora-tory settings may not appropriately capture real-life problems and their solutions. However, the strict design of experiments offers falsifiable evi-dence about which aspects of the prior context are relevant for the advisee's interpretations. Using corpus results to generate hypotheses for experiments is therefore a good additional step. Multimodal cues of advice or speech act solicitation and uptake provide another resource on which to draw. The lack of video recordings in LLC meant that the use of gaze, hand gestures, and facial expressions to indicate solicitation or acceptance (or not) remain hidden to us. However, the growing number of corpus pragmatic studies involving multimodality points to a clear shift in the field's focus from verbal to non-verbal.

6 Conclusion

This Element has made a contribution to a new generation of corpus prag-matics research through a detailed empirical investigation of advice in natural conversation. What is original about this approach is its consider-ation of different ways of investigating speech acts by means of corpus methods, as reflected in the synergies across theoretical, qualitative, quanti-tative, and statistical approaches applied to corpus data of spoken dialogue across time. The approach is a response to much research in corpus prag-matics that uses large, multimillion-word corpora and numbers from off-the-shelf software tools without taking into consideration the subtleties of dialogic interaction and the interlocutor's behaviour relative to each other. At the same time, it avoids making broad generalisations about the commu-nicative functions of pragmatic phenomena based on few examples from restricted settings. The answer for corpus pragmatics, then, is to keep up with the rapid expansion of statistical modelling in the language sciences more generally, and to incorporate into the models the range of dialogic and sequential factors that affect people's pragmatic choices in real communica-tion. The growing number of studies in pragmatics that do exactly that is a step in the right direction. Due to its reliance on naturally occurring data, corpus pragmatics would also profit from taking advantage of the growing availability of spoken corpora. The LLC of spoken British English, compris-ing LLC–1 from the 1950s to 1980s and the new LLC–2 from 2014 to 2019, proved to be a useful resource for the analysis of advice both from a synchronic and a diachronic perspective.

Advice is a major topic within conversation analytic and interactional linguistic approaches to social interaction, and yet there are gaps in our knowledge about the social actions of advice-giving and advice uptake in conversation. We have sought to contribute to some of them. Based on a large number of corpus examples, we found systematic differences in the way advice is given in conversations between equals (casual conversation) and conversations between disparates (institutional conversation), with the former being characterised by more direct forms of advising due to reduced face concerns among people who are not constrained by institutional affiliations. More forceful types of advice constructions also seem to have become more acceptable in the present day. But, considering that this is the first diachronic study on advice-giving in recent history, we need more evidence from different sources to be able to argue for or against the democratisation hypothesis (see Põldvere, forthcoming). The investigation of advice uptake relative to a range of constructional, dialogic, and social factors revealed strong associations with many of them. We have shown that, although (non-)solicitation has an effect on uptake, *who* gives the advice and *how* it is given matter more. The effect of constructional choice, in particular, can have interesting implications for situations where speakers find themselves needing to dispense unsolicited advice, whether in formal or informal contexts, and have strong reasons to wish for it to be heeded. All in all, then, these results point to diverse frames of advice exchanges with different advice outcomes. The high rates of resistance, rejection, and other responses (such as silence) in many of the advice frames, however, lead us to believe that, sometimes, no advice is the best advice.

In the Introduction, we framed our Element with respect to two funda-mental collaborative motives of human socialising posited by Tomasello (2008), namely, helping and sharing. Clearly, both motives are emblematic of advice. The essence of advice is to help others by sharing information that we think might be beneficial for them. These basic human communicative motives are invoked by a rich and complex set of particular social intentions in particular contexts, conveyed through specific form–meaning pairings, and they carry profound implications for the advice situation. No single approach, theoretical or methodological, is powerful enough to account for such complex human social behaviour. Put another way, if giving and responding to advice is no easy feat, why would understanding it be any different?

References

Adolphs, S. (2008). *Corpus and Context: Investigating Pragmatic Functions in Spoken Discourse*. Amsterdam: John Benjamins.

Aijmer, K. (1996). *Conversational Routines in English: Convention and Creativity*. London: Routledge.

Aijmer, K. (2018). Corpus pragmatics: From form to function. In A. Jucker, K. Schneider & W. Bublitz, eds., *Methods in Pragmatics*. Berlin: De Gruyter Mouton, pp. 555–585.

Aijmer, K. & Rühlemann, C., eds. (2015). *Corpus Pragmatics: A Handbook*. Cambridge: Cambridge University Press.

Archer, D. & Culpeper, J. (2018). Pragmatic annotation. In A. Jucker, K. Schneider & W. Bublitz, eds., *Methods in Pragmatics*. Berlin: De Gruyter Mouton, pp. 493–525.

Arundale, R. (2010). Constituting face in conversation: Face, facework and interactional achievement. *Journal of Pragmatics*, **42**(8), 2078–2105.

Austin, J. L. (1962). *How to Do Things with Words*. Cambridge, MA: Harvard University Press.

Bowie, J., Wallis, S. & Aarts, B. (2013). Contemporary change in modal usage in spoken British English: Mapping the impact of "genre". In J. Marín-Arrese, M. Carretero, J. Arús Hita & J. van der Auwera, eds., *English Modality: Core, Periphery and Evidentiality*. Berlin: De Gruyter Mouton, pp. 57–94.

Brown, P. & Levinson. S. (1987). *Politeness: Some Universals in Language Usage*. Cambridge: Cambridge University Press.

Butler, C., Potter, J., Danby, S., Emmison, M. & Hepburn, A. (2010). Advice-implicative interrogatives: Building "client-centered" support in a children's helpline. *Social Psychology Quarterly*, **73**(3), 265–287.

Clancy, B. & O'Keeffe, A. (2015). Pragmatics. In D. Biber & R. Reppen, eds., *The Cambridge Handbook of Corpus Linguistics*. Cambridge: Cambridge University Press, pp. 235–251.

Clark, H. (1996). *Using Language*. Cambridge: Cambridge University Press.

Close, J. & Aarts, B. (2010). Current change in the modal system of English: A case study of *must*, *have to* and *have got to*. In U. Lenker, J. Huber & R. Mailhammer, eds., *The History of English Verbal and Nominal Constructions*. Amsterdam: John Benjamins, pp. 165–181.

Cohen, J. (1960). A coefficient of agreement for nominal scales. *Educational and Psychological Measurement*, **20**, 37–46.

Couper-Kuhlen, E. (2014). What does grammar tell us about action? *Pragmatics*, **24**(3), 623–647.

Couper-Kuhlen, E. & Thompson, S. (2022). Action ascription and deonticity in everyday advice-giving sequences. In A. Deppermann & M. Haugh, eds., *Action Ascription in Interaction*. Cambridge: Cambridge University Press, pp. 183–207.

Cruttenden, A. (1997). *Intonation*. Cambridge: Cambridge University Press.

Culpeper, J. (2016). Impoliteness strategies. In A. Capone & J. Mey, eds., *Interdisciplinary Studies in Pragmatics, Culture and Society*. New York: Springer, pp. 421–445.

Culpeper, J. & Archer, D. (2008). Requests and directness in early modern English trial proceedings and play-texts, 1640–1760. In A. Jucker & I. Taavitsainen, eds., *Speech Acts in the History of English*. Amsterdam: John Benjamins, pp. 45–84.

Culpeper, J. & Demmen, J. (2011). Nineteenth-century English politeness: Negative politeness, conventional indirect requests and the rise of the individual self. *Journal of Historical Pragmatics*, **12**(1–2), 49–81.

Culpeper, J. & Haugh, M. (2014). *Pragmatics and the English Language*. Basingstoke: Palgrave Macmillan.

De Felice, R. (2013). A corpus-based classification of commitments in business English. In J. Romero-Trillo, ed., *Yearbook of Corpus Linguistics and Pragmatics Vol 1*. New York: Springer, pp. 153–171.

De Felice, R., Darby, J., Fisher, A. & Peplow, D. (2013). A classification scheme for annotating speech acts in a business email corpus. *ICAME Journal*, **37**, 71–106.

De Smedt, T. & Daelemans, W. (2012). Pattern for Python. *Journal of Machine Learning Research*, **13**, 2031–2035.

Deutschmann, M. (2003). *Apologising in British English*. Ph.D. dissertation, Umeå University.

Diederich, C. & Höhn, N. (2012). "Well it's not for me to advise you, of course … ". *Advice* and *advise* in the British National Corpus of English. In H. Limberg & M. Locher, eds., *Advice in Discourse*. Amsterdam: John Benjamins, pp. 333–358.

Eelen, G. (2001). *A Critique of Politeness Theories*. Manchester: St. Jerome.

Facchinetti, R., Palmer, F. & Krug, M., eds. (2003). *Modality in Contemporary English*. Berlin: De Gruyter Mouton.

Fauconnier, G. (1994). *Mental Spaces: Aspects of Meaning Construction in Natural Language*. Cambridge: Cambridge University Press.

Figueras Bates, C. (2020). Cognitive and affective dimensions of mitigation in advice. *Corpus Pragmatics*, **4**, 31–57

Fillmore, C. J. (1982) Frame semantics. In The Linguistic Society of Korea, eds., *Linguistics in the Morning Calm*. Seoul: Hanshin, pp. 111–137.

Fillmore, C. J. & Baker, C. F. (2009). A frames approach to semantic analysis. In B. Heine & H. Narrog, eds, *The Oxford Handbook of Linguistic Analysis*. Oxford: Oxford University Press, pp. 313–340.

Fitzmaurice, S. & Taavitsainen, I. (2007). *Methods in Historical Pragmatics*. Berlin: De Gruyter Mouton.

Flöck, I., & Geluykens, R. (2018). Preference organization and cross-cultural variation in request responses. *Corpus Pragmatics*, **2**, 57–82.

Goffman, E. (1967). *Interaction Ritual: Essays on Face-to-Face Behavior*. New York: Pantheon Books.

Goldberg, A. (2006). *Constructions at Work*. Oxford: Oxford University Press.

Goldsmith, D. (2000). Soliciting advice: The role of sequential placement in mitigating face threat. *Communications Monographs*, **67**(1), 1–19.

Greenbaum. S. & Svartvik, J. (1990). *The London-Lund Corpus of Spoken English*. Lund: Lund University Press.

Grice, H. P. (1975). Logic and conversation. In P. Cole & J. L. Morgan, eds., *Syntax and Semantics Vol. 3*. New York: Academic Press, pp. 41–58.

Gries, S. Th. (2015a). Statistics for learner corpus research. In G. Gilquin, S. Granger & F. Meunier, eds., *The Cambridge Handbook of Learner Corpus Research*. Cambridge: Cambridge University Press, pp. 159–181.

Gries, S. Th. (2015b). The most underused statistical method in corpus linguistics: Multi-level (and mixed-effects) models. *Corpora*, **10**(1), 95–125.

Gries, S. Th. (2019). On classification trees and random forests in corpus linguistics: Some words of caution and suggestions for improvement. *Corpus Linguistics and Linguistic Theory*, **16**(3), 617–647.

Haugh, M. (2014). *Im/Politeness Implicatures*. Berlin: De Gruyter Mouton.

Haugh, M. (2017). Prompting offers of assistance in interaction. *Pragmatics and Society*, **8**(2), 183–207.

Haugh, M. & Culpeper, J. (2018). Integrative pragmatics and (im)politeness theory. In C. Ilie & N. Norrick, eds., *Pragmatics and its Interfaces*. Amsterdam: John Benjamins, pp. 213–239.

Hepburn, A. & Potter, J. (2011). Designing the recipient: Managing advice resistance in institutional settings. *Social Psychology Quarterly*, **74**(2), 216–241.

Heritage, J. (2012). The epistemic engine: Sequence organization and territories of knowledge. *Research on Language and Social Interaction*, **45**(1), 30–52.

Heritage, J. & Sefi, S. (1992). Dilemmas of advice: Aspects of the delivery and reception of advice in interactions between health visitors and first-time mothers. In P. Drew & J. Heritage, eds., *Talk at Work: Interaction in Institutional Settings*. Cambridge: Cambridge University Press, pp. 359–417.

Hommerberg, C. & Paradis, C. (2014). Constructing credibility in wine reviews. Evidentiality, temporality and epistemic control. In D. Glynn & M. Sjölin, eds., *Subjectivity and Epistemicity*. Lund: Lund University Press, pp. 211–238.

Hudson, T. (1990). The discourse of advice giving in English: "I wouldn't feed until spring no matter what you do". *Language & Communication*, **10**(4), 285–297.

Hutchby, I. (1995). Aspects of recipient design in expert advice-giving on call-in radio. *Discourse Processes*, **19**(2), 219–238.

Jautz, S. (2013). *Thanking Formulae in English: Explorations across Varieties and Genres*. Amsterdam: John Benjamins.

Jefferson, G. & Lee, J. (1981). The rejection of advice: Managing the problematic convergence of a "troubles-telling" and a "service encounter". *Journal of Pragmatics*, **5**(5), 399–421.

Jucker, A. (2018). Introduction to part 5: Corpus pragmatics. In A. H. Jucker, K. P. Schneider & W. Bublitz, eds., *Methods in Pragmatics*. Berlin: De Gruyter Mouton, pp. 455–466.

Jucker, A. (2020). *Politeness in the History of English: From the Middle Ages to the Present Day*. Cambridge: Cambridge University Press.

Jucker, A. & Kopaczyk, J. (2017). Historical (Im)politeness. In J. Culpeper, M. Haugh & D. Kádár, eds., *The Palgrave Handbook of Linguistic (Im) politeness*. London: Palgrave Macmillan.

Jucker, A., Schneider, K. & Bublitz, W., eds. (2018). *Methods in Pragmatics*. Berlin: De Gruyter Mouton.

Jucker, A., Schneider, G., Taavitsainen, I. & Breustedt, B. (2008). Fishing for compliments: Precision and recall in corpus-linguistic compliment research. In A. Jucker & I. Taavitsainen, eds., *Speech Acts in the History of English*. Amsterdam: John Benjamins, pp. 273–294.

Jucker, A. & Taavitsainen, I. (2008). *Speech Acts in the History of English*. Amsterdam: John Benjamins.

Kádár, D. & Haugh, M. (2013). *Understanding Politeness*. Cambridge: Cambridge University Press.

Kinnell, A. & Maynard, D. (1996). The delivery and receipt of safer sex advice in pretest counseling sessions for HIV and AIDS. *Journal of Contemporary Ethnography*, **24**(4), 405–437.

Klavan, J., Pilvik, M. & Uiboaed, K. (2015). The use of multivariate statistical classification models for predicting constructional choice in spoken, non-standard varieties of Estonian. *SKY Journal of Linguistics*, **28**, 187–224.

Lakoff, R. (1973). The logic of politeness; or minding your p's and q's. *Chicago Linguistics Society*, **9**, 292–305.

Landis, J. R. & Koch, G. (1977). An application of hierarchical Kappa-type statistics in the assessment of majority agreement among multiple observers. *Biometrics*, **33**(2), 363–374.

Larsson, T., Callies, M., Hasselgård, H. *et al.* (2020). Adverb placement in EFL academic writing: Going beyond syntactic transfer. *International Journal of Corpus Linguistics*, **25**(2), 155–184.

Leech, G. (1983). *Principles of Pragmatics*. London: Longman.

Leech, G. (2014). *The Pragmatics of Politeness*. Oxford: Oxford University Press.

Leech, G., Hundt, M., Mair, C. & Smith, N. (2009). *Change in Contemporary English: A Grammatical Study*. Cambridge: Cambridge University Press.

Levinson, S. (1983). *Pragmatics*. Cambridge: Cambridge University Press.

Levshina, N. (2015). *How to Do Linguistics with R: Data Exploration and Statistical Analysis*. Amsterdam: John Benjamins.

Levshina, N. (2021). Conditional inference trees and random forests. In M. Paquot & S. Th. Gries, eds., *Practical Handbook of Corpus Linguistics*. New York: Springer, pp. 611–643.

Limberg, H. & Locher, M., eds. (2012). *Advice in Discourse*. Amsterdam: John Benjamins.

Locher, M. (2006). Polite behaviour within relational work. The discursive approach to politeness. *Multilingua*, **25**(3), 249–267.

Locher, M. (2013). Internet advice. In S. Herring, D. Stein & T. Virtanen, eds., *Pragmatics of Computer-Mediated Communication*. Berlin: De Gruyter Mouton, pp. 339–362.

Love, R. & Curry, N. (2021). Recent change in modality in informal spoken British English: 1990s–2010s. *English Language and Linguistics*, **25**(3), 537–562.

Lutzky, U. & Kehoe, A. (2016). "Oops, I didn't mean to be so flippant". A corpus pragmatic analysis of apologies in blog data. *Journal of Pragmatics*, **116**, 27–36.

MacGeorge, E. L., Feng, B., Butler, G. & Budarz, S. (2004). Understanding advice in supportive interactions. *Human Communication Research*, **30**(1), 42–70.

MacGeorge, E. L., Guntzviller, L., Branch, S. & Yakova, L. (2016). Paths of resistance: An interpretive analysis of trajectories in less satisfying advice interactions. *Journal of Language and Social Psychology*, **35**(5), 548–568.

MacGeorge, E. L., Lichtman, R. & Pressey, L. (2002). The evaluation of advice in supportive interactions: Facework and contextual factors. *Human Communication Research*, **28**(3), 451–463.

MacGeorge, E. L. & Van Swol, L. M., eds. (2018). *The Oxford Handbook of Advice*. Oxford: Oxford University Press.

Mair, C. & Leech, G. (2020). Current changes in English syntax. In B. Aarts, A. McMahon & L. Hinrich, eds., *The Handbook of English Linguistics*. Malden: Wiley Blackwell, pp. 249–276.

Marín–Arrese, J., Carretero, M., Arús Hita, J. & van der Auwera, J., eds. (2013). *English Modality: Core, Periphery and Evidentiality*. Berlin: De Gruyter Mouton.

Mills, S. (2003). *Gender and Politeness*. Cambridge: Cambridge University Press.

Murphy, M. L. & De Felice, R. (2019). Routine politeness in American and British English requests: Use and non-use of *please*. *Journal of Politeness Research*, **15**(1), 77–100.

Oben, B. & Brône, G. (2016). Explaining interactive alignment: A multimodal and multifactorial account. *Journal of Pragmatics*, **104**, 32–51.

Paradis, C. (2003a). Is the notion of *linguistic competence* relevant in Cognitive Linguistics? *Annual Review of Cognitive Linguistics*, **1**, 207–231.

Paradis, C. (2003b). Between epistemic modality and degree: The case of *really*. In R. Facchinetti, F. Palmer & M. Krug, eds., *Modality in Contemporary English*. Berlin: De Gruyter Mouton, pp. 191–222.

Paradis, C. (2009). "This beauty should drink well for 10–12 years": A note on recommendations as semantic middles. *Text & Talk*, **29**(1), 53–73.

Paradis, C. (2011). Metonymization: Key mechanism in language change. In R. Benczes, A. Barcelona & F. Ruiz de Mendoza Ibáñez, eds., *Defining Metonymy in Cognitive Linguistics*. Amsterdam: John Benjamins, pp. 61–88.

Paradis, C. (2015). Meanings of words: Theory and application. In U. Hass & P. Storjohann, eds., *Handbuch Wort und Wortschatz*. Berlin: De Gruyter Mouton, pp. 274–294.

Paradis, C. (2020). Two layers of modal grounding of recommendations. In V. Kloudová, M. Šemelik, A. Racochová & T. Koptik, eds., *Spielräume der Modernen Linguistischen Forschung*. Prague: The Karolinum Press, pp. 112–127.

Põldvere, N. (forthcoming). Recent change of modality in one speech act in spoken English. *Journal of English Linguistics*.

Põldvere, N., Frid, J., Johansson, V. & Paradis, C. (2021). Challenges of releasing audio material for spoken data: The case of the London–Lund Corpus 2. *Research in Corpus Linguistics*, **9**(1), 35–62.

Põldvere, N., Fuoli, M. & Paradis, C. (2016). A study of dialogic expansion and contraction in spoken discourse using corpus and experimental techniques. *Corpora*, **11**(2), 191–225.

Põldvere, N., Johansson, V. & Paradis, C. (2021). On the London–Lund Corpus 2: Design, challenges and innovations. *English Language and Linguistics*, **25**(3), 459–483.

Põldvere, N. & Paradis, C. (2019). Motivations and mechanisms for the development of the reactive *what-x* construction in spoken dialogue. *Journal of Pragmatics*, **143**, 65–84.

Põldvere, N. & Paradis, C. (2020). "What and then a little robot brings it to you?" The reactive *what-x* construction is spoken dialogue. *English Language and Linguistics*, **24**(2), 307–332.

Pudlinski, C. (2002). Accepting and rejecting advice as competent peers: Caller dilemmas on a warm line. *Discourse Studies*, **4**(4), 481–500.

Quirk, R., Greenbaum, S., Leech, G. & Svartvik, J. (1985). *A Comprehensive Grammar of the English Language*. London: Longman.

Rautionaho, P. & Hundt, M. (2021). Primed progressives? Predicting aspectual choice in World Englishes. *Corpus Linguistics and Linguistic Theory*. https://doi.org/10.1515/cllt-2021-0012

Romero-Trillo, J. (2017). Corpus pragmatics. *Corpus Pragmatics*, **1**, 1–2.

Ronan, P. (2015). Categorizing expressive speech acts in the pragmatically annotated SPICE Ireland corpus. *ICAME Journal*, **39**, 25–45.

RStudio Team. (2020). RStudio: Integrated Development for R. RStudio, PBC, Boston, MA. https://rstudio.com/

Rühlemann, C. (2017). Integrating corpus-linguistic and conversation-analytic transcription in XML: The case of backchannels and overlap in storytelling interaction. *Corpus Pragmatics*, **1**(3), 201–232.

Rühlemann, C. (2019). *Corpus Linguistics for Pragmatics: A Guide for Research*. Abingdon: Routledge.

Rühlemann, C. & Gries, S. Th. (2020). Speakers advance-project turn completion by slowing down: A multifactorial corpus analysis. *Journal of Phonetics*, **80**, 100976.

Rühlemann, C. & Gries, S. Th. (2021). How do speakers and hearers disambiguate multi-functional words? The case of *well*. *Functions of Language*, **28**(1), 55–80.

Searle, J. R. (1969). *Speech Acts: An Essay in the Philosophy of Language*. Cambridge: Cambridge University Press.

Searle, J. R. (1976). A classification of illocutionary acts. *Language in Society*, **5**(1), 1–23.

Seitanidi, E., Põldvere, N. & Paradis, C. (forthcoming). *All*-cleft constructions in the London–Lund Corpora of spoken English: Methodological and empirical perspectives. *Journal of Pragmatics*.

Shaw, C. & Hepburn, A. (2013). Managing the moral implications of advice in informal interaction. *Research on Language and Social Interaction*, **46**(4), 344–362.

Shaw, C., Potter, J. & Hepburn, A. (2015). Advice-implicative actions: Using interrogatives and assessments to deliver advice in mundane conversation. *Discourse Studies*, **17**(3), 317–342.

Smith, N. (2003). Changes in the modals and semi-modals of strong obligation and epistemic necessity in recent British English. In R. Facchinetti, F. Palmer, & M. Krug, eds., *Modality in Contemporary English*. Berlin: De Gruyter Mouton, pp. 241–266.

Smith, N. & Leech, G. (2013). Verb structures in twentieth-century British English. In B. Aarts, J. Close, G. Leech & S. Wallis, eds., *The Verb Phrase in English*. Cambridge: Cambridge University Press, pp. 68–98.

Stivers, T., Heritage, J., Barnes, R. *et al.* (2018). Treatment recommendations as actions. *Health Communication*, **33**(11), 1335–1344.

Strobl, C., Boulesteix, A. L., Kneib, T., Augustin, T. & Zeileis, A. (2008). Conditional variable importance for random forests. *BMC Bioinformatics*, **9**, 307.

Svartvik, J. & Quirk, R. (1980). *A Corpus of English Conversation*. Lund: Lund University Press.

Szmrecsanyi, B., Grafmiller, J., Heller, B. & Röthlisberger, M. (2016). Around the world in three alternations: Modeling syntactic variation in varieties of English. *English World-Wide*, **37**(2), 109–137.

Taavitsainen, I. (2018). Historical corpus pragmatics. In A. H. Jucker, K. P. Schneider & W. Bublitz, eds., *Methods in Pragmatics*. Berlin: De Gruyter Mouton, pp. 527–554.

Taavitsainen, I., Jucker, A. & Tuominen, J., eds. (2014). *Diachronic Corpus Pragmatics*. Amsterdam: John Benjamins.

Tagliamonte, S. & Baayen, R. H. (2012). Models, forests, and trees of York English: *Was/were* variation as a case study for statistical practice. *Language Variation and Change*, **24**(2), 135–178.

Tantucci, V. & Wang, A. (2018). Illocutional concurrences: The case of evaluative speech acts and face-work in spoken Mandarin and American English. *Journal of Pragmatics*, **138**, 60–76.

Tantucci, V. & Wang, A. (2021). Resonance and engagement through (dis-) agreement: Evidence of persistent constructional priming from Mandarin naturalistic interaction. *Journal of Pragmatics*, **175**, 94–111.

Tantucci, V. & Wang, A. (2022). Dynamic resonance and explicit dialogic engagement in Mandarin first language acquisition. *Discourse Processes.* https://doi.org/10.1080/0163853X.2022.2065175

Terkourafi, M. (2002). Politeness and formulaicity: Evidence from Cypriot Greek. *Journal of Greek Linguistics*, **3**, 179–201.

Terkourafi, M. (2005). Beyond the micro-level in politeness research. *Journal of Politeness Research*, **1**, 237–262.

Terkourafi, M. (2015). Conventionalization: A new agenda for im/politeness research. *Journal of Pragmatics*, **86**, 11–18.

Tomasello, M. (2008). *Origins of Human Communication*. Cambridge, MA: MIT Press.

van der Auwera, J. & De Wit, A. (2010). The English comparative modals – A pilot study. In B. Cappelle & N. Waka, eds., *Distinctions in English Grammar, Offered to Renaat Declerck*. Tokyo: Kaitakusha, pp. 127–147.

Van Olmen, D. & Tantucci, V. (2022). Getting attention in different languages: A usage-based approach to parenthetical LOOK in Chinese, Dutch, English and Italian. *Intercultural Pragmatics*, **19**(2), 141–181.

Van Swol, L., Paik, J., & Prahl, A. (2018). Advice recipients: The psychology of advice utilization. In E. L. MacGeorge & L. van Swol, eds., *The Oxford Handbook of Advice*. Oxford: Oxford University Press, pp. 21–41.

Vehviläinen, S. (2001). Evaluative advice in educational counseling: The use of disagreement in the "stepwise entry" to advice. *Research on Language and Social Interaction*, **34**, 371–398.

Waring, H. (2007). The multi-functionality of accounts in advice giving. *Journal of Sociolinguistics*, **11**(3), 367–391.

Watts, R. (2003). *Politeness*. Cambridge: Cambridge University Press.

Weisser, M. (2019). The DART annotation scheme: Form, applicability & application. *Studia Neophilologica*, **91**(2), 131–153.

Wichmann, A. (2004). The intonation of *Please*-requests: A corpus-based study. *Journal of Pragmatics*, **36**(9), 1521–1549.

Acknowledgements

This work has been made possible by generous financial support from a number of institutions and funders. We are grateful for the funding provided by the Crafoord Foundation for Nele Põldvere's postdoctoral project, the Survey of English Usage at University College London for a research assistant, and the Olof Sager Foundation and the Centre for Languages and Literature at Lund University for our research trips. We are also grateful for the help provided by Christy Wensley (annotations) and Tove Larsson (statistics) as well as to the editors of this series and the two anonymous reviewers for their constructive comments on the earlier version of the manuscript.

Cambridge Elements ☰

Pragmatics

Jonathan Culpeper
Lancaster University

Jonathan Culpeper is Professor of English Language and Linguistics in the Department of Linguistics and English Language at Lancaster University, UK. A former co-editor-in-chief of the *Journal of Pragmatics* (2009–14), with research spanning multiple areas within pragmatics, his major publications include: *Impoliteness: Using Language to Cause Offence* (2011, CUP) and *Pragmatics and the English Language* (2014, Palgrave; with Michael Haugh).

Michael Haugh
University of Queensland, Australia

Michael Haugh is Professor of Linguistics and Applied Linguistics in the School of Languages and Cultures at the University of Queensland, Australia. A former co-editor-in-chief of the *Journal of Pragmatics* (2015–2020), with research spanning multiple areas within pragmatics, his major publications include: *Understanding Politeness* (2013, CUP; with Dániel Kádár), *Pragmatics and the English Language* (2014, Palgrave; with Jonathan Culpeper), and *Im/politeness Implicatures* (2015, Mouton de Gruyter).

About the Series
The Cambridge Elements in Pragmatics series showcases dynamic and high-quality original, concise and accessible scholarly works. Written for a broad pragmatics readership it encourages dialogue across different perspectives on language use. It is a forum for cutting-edge work in pragmatics: consolidating theory (especially through cross-fertilization), leading the development of new methods, and advancing innovative topics in pragmatics.

Cambridge Elements ☰

Pragmatics

Elements in the Series

Advice in Conversation: Corpus Pragmatics Meets Mixed Methods
Nele Põldvere, Rachele De Felice and Carita Paradis

A full series listing is available at: www.cambridge.org/EIPR

Printed in the United States
by Baker & Taylor Publisher Services